D0422959

All Things

are working for your

Good

Also by Joel Osteen

DAILY READINGS
— from —

All Things
are working for your
Good

#1 *New York Times* Bestselling Author

JOEL OSTEEN

Faith
Words

New York • Nashville

Copyright © 2018 by Joel Osteen

Hachette Book Group supports the right to free expression and the value of copyright. The purpose of copyright is to encourage writers and artists to produce the creative works that enrich our culture. The scanning, uploading, and electronic sharing of any part of this book without the permission of the publisher is unlawful piracy and theft of the author's intellectual property. If you would like to use material from the book (other than for review purposes), prior written permission must be obtained by contacting the publisher at permissions@hbgusa.com. Thank you for your support of the author's rights.

Unless otherwise noted, all Scripture quotations are taken from *The Holy Bible, New International Version*® NIV®. Copyright © 1973, 1978, 1984, 2011 by Biblica, Inc.™ Used by permission. All rights reserved worldwide.

Scripture quotations noted NKJV are taken from the *New King James Version* of the Bible. Copyright © 1982 by Thomas Nelson, Inc. Used by permission. All rights reserved.

Scripture quotations noted NLT are taken from the *Holy Bible, New Living Translation*, copyright © 1996, 2004, 2007 by Tyndale House Foundation. Used by permission of Tyndale House Publishers, Inc., Carol Stream, IL 60188. All rights reserved.

Scripture quotations noted AMP are taken from *The Amplified Bible*. Copyright © 2015 by The Lockman Foundation, La Habra, CA 90631. All rights reserved. For permission to quote information visit www.lockman.org..

Scripture quotations noted AMPC are taken from *The Amplified Bible Classic Edition*. Copyright © 1954, 1958, 1962, 1964, 1965, 1987 by The Lockman Foundation, La Habra, CA 90631. All rights reserved. For permission to quote information visit www.lockman.org.

Scriptures noted TLB are taken from *The Living Bible*, copyright © 1971. Used by permission of Tyndale House Publishers, Inc., Carol Stream, IL 60188. All rights reserved.

Scriptures noted MSG are taken from *The Message*. Copyright © 1993, 1994, 1995, 1996, 2000, 2001, 2002. Used by permission of NavPress Publishing Group.

Scripture quotations noted ESV are taken from the *The Holy Bible, English Standard Version*®. Copyright © 2001 by Crossway, a publishing ministry of Good News Publishers. ESV® Text Edition: 2011. Used by permission. All rights reserved.

Scripture quotations noted KJV are from the *King James Version* of the Holy Bible.

Literary development: Lance Wubbels Literary Services, Bloomington, Minnesota.

FaithWords
Hachette Book Group
1290 Avenue of the Americas
New York, NY 10104
faithwords.com
twitter.com/faithwords

First Edition: November 2018
10 9 8 7 6 5 4 3 2 1

FaithWords is a division of Hachette Book Group, Inc.
The FaithWords name and logo are trademarks of Hachette Book Group, Inc.

The Hachette Speakers Bureau provides a wide range of authors for speaking events. To find out more, go to www.hachettespeakersbureau.com or call (866) 376-6591.

The publisher is not responsible for websites (or their content) that are not owned by the publisher.

ISBN: 978-1-5460-3302-8 (paper over board), 978-1-5460-3305-9 (ebook)

Printed in the United States of America

LSC-C

. . . . . .

And we know that all things

work together for good

to those who love God,

to those who are the called

according to His purpose.

Romans 8:28 NKJV

Introduction

. . . .

All of us will go through negative things that we don't like or understand, such as loss, sickness, or divorce. Those experiences are a part of the human journey. But when we find ourselves in such difficult places, it's easy to get discouraged, give up on our dreams, and just settle.

We may not realize it, but when we feel buried in difficulties, we have great reasons to be encouraged. God wouldn't have allowed the difficulties unless He was going to use them to cause us to grow and reach our highest potential. Those obstacles and challenges are all a part of His plan to make us into who we were created to be. That's where our character is developed. If we stay in faith and keep a good attitude when we go through challenges, we will not only grow, but we will see how God works all things together for our good.

That is why I wrote this devotional—to help you harness insights from *All Things Are*

Working for Your Good and to focus on how to trust God when life doesn't make sense. It will help you understand that there are seeds of talent, potential, and greatness buried deep within you that will only come to life in the dark times. As you learn to trust Him to be with you through the difficulties, it's just a matter of time before you break out and blossom into your full potential. I hope that these devotions will inspire you each day, and they will help you overcome the challenges or barriers that might keep you from discovering your best life possible.

Your life can be transformed and renewed as you allow God's Word to refresh and to reshape your thinking, speaking, and daily activities. You will find a wealth of Scriptures and points for contemplation. Allow the Scriptures to speak to your heart. Be still and listen to what God is saying to you. Day by day, the barriers that hold you back will begin to loosen and fall off your life.

No matter what challenges or troubles you face, God has it all figured out. He can see things you can't see. His ways are better than our ways. God has promised, "I'm going to cause good things to work out that you could never make happen on your own." Discover the keys to knowing that God is always for you, that it's all good, and becoming the person of faith and character God designed you to be, even when hope seems impossible.

DAILY READINGS
— *from* —

All Things
are working for your
Good

All Things
are working for your
Good

Strength of Heart

*My flesh and my heart
may fail, but God is the
strength of my heart and
my portion forever.*

Psalm 73:26

Life is full of things that we don't like—
we get disappointed, a friend betrays us,
we didn't get the promotion that we worked
so hard for. We see these things as being
negative, thinking, *That was bad. It didn't
work out. My prayers didn't get answered.* It's
easy to get discouraged and lose our passion.

But God won't allow a difficulty unless
He's going to somehow use it for our good.
If you'll keep the right attitude, everything
that happens in life will push you further
into your destiny. This includes the closed
doors you face, the delays, and the loan
that didn't go through. God says, "It's all
good. I'm in control. It may not feel good,
but if you'll trust Me, I'm going to use it
for your good."

It's All Good

Good sense makes one slow to anger, and it is his glory to overlook an offense.

Proverbs 19:11 ESV

When you understand the principle that God is going to use difficulties for your good, life gets much more freeing. You don't get upset when a coworker plays politics and leaves you out. You know it's all good. God allowed it, and He's going to use it. You tried, and the business didn't make it. You don't give up on your dreams. You know it's all good. It's a part of the process. You don't let simple things, such as getting stuck in traffic, get you frustrated and ruin your day. You know that God is directing your steps. By slowing you down, He may be keeping you from an accident. He may be developing patience in you. Whatever it is, He has a purpose for it. Keep the right perspective: it's all good.

Protected

You hem me in behind and before, and you lay your hand upon me.

Psalm 139:5

We're not going to understand everything that happens and doesn't happen in our lives. If you try to figure it all out, you'll get frustrated. God can see the big picture for our lives. He knows where the dead ends are, the shortcuts, the bumpy roads that are going to cause you heartache and pain. He'll keep doors closed that you prayed would open, because He knows going through them would be a waste of your time. God is asking, "Do you trust Me with your closed doors? Do you trust Me with your unanswered prayers?"

When you're mature, instead of getting bitter when things don't work out, you'll say, "God, I trust You. I may not like it, but I believe You know what's best for me."

Be Faithful

*In everything you do, stay away from
complaining and arguing...*

Philippians 2:14 TLB

Some of the things that God has in your
future you wouldn't be able to handle
if He gave them to you right now. He loves
you too much to let that happen. He's
developing your character, growing you up.
That boss who gets on your nerves, who
doesn't treat you right—you keep trying to
pray him away. The reason he's not going
away is that God is using him like sandpaper
to rub the rough edges off you. As you keep
doing the right thing, keeping your mouth
closed, being respectful, being faithful to
your responsibilities, that's doing a work in
you. You couldn't develop your character
without him.

You may not like it, but it's good. It's
getting you ready for the next level of your
destiny.

To Your Advantage

*All things work together for good
to those who love God.*

Romans 8:28 NKJV

If you're fighting everything you don't like,
you need to have this new perspective:
it's all good. Whether it's a grouchy boss,
an illness you're dealing with, or a dream
that's taking forever to be fulfilled, you can
say, "I don't like how this has gone, but
God is on the throne. He promised that
He would use what has come against me to
my advantage." *All things* work together for
good. They may not be good at the time we
go through them. It's painful to go through
a loss. It hurts when people do us wrong.
It's discouraging when a dream doesn't work
out. By themselves, they may not be good,
but God promises He's going to bring it all
together. One day you'll look back and say
that it was all good.

Have a Victor's Mentality

6

No, in all these things we are more than conquerors through him who loved us.

Romans 8:37

You may feel discouraged because you lost a loved one or because a business partner cheated you, and you're saying those things weren't good. The problem is that you're isolating single incidents. God hasn't brought them together yet. That setback was a setup for God to show out in your life. You have to get rid of the victim mentality and start having a victor mentality. When you have this attitude that it's all good, you don't go around with a chip on your shoulder. You know God has you in the palms of His hands. You have a spring in your step because you know it's just a matter of time before God brings it all together. Scripture says that weeping may endure for a night, but joy comes in the morning.

From Worst to Best

*"...but we had hoped that he
was the one who was going
to redeem Israel."*

Luke 24:21

We celebrate Good Friday each year. We call it "good" now, but on the day when Jesus was crucified, the disciples thought it was the worst day of their lives. Their dreams were shattered. The Man Whom they had devoted their lives to had been crucified, was dead, and had been buried in a tomb. Doubts filled their minds.

But a few days later, when Jesus rose from the dead and appeared to them in the upper room, they realized that He was Who He'd said He was. He had done what He'd said He was going to do. He'd defeated the enemy and brought salvation to mankind. When they looked back on that Friday, what they'd thought was the worst day of their lives they now called "good."

Good Friday

…with the doors locked for fear of the Jewish leaders, Jesus came and stood among [the disciples] and said, "Peace be with you!"

John 20:19

*G*ood is the last word the disciples would have used to describe the Friday when Jesus was crucified. *Tragic Friday* would have seemed like a more accurate description. However, after Jesus rose from the dead, they looked back on that Friday and said, "It wasn't what we thought. It wasn't tragic Friday. It was all a part of His plan. It was Good Friday."

We all face times when a dream dies, a relationship ends, we come down with an illness—nothing about the situation seems good. It may not be good right now, but God knows how to bring it all together. You may think it is going to stop you, set you back, and cause you heartache. If you'll stay in faith, one day you'll look back and say it was good.

January 9

There Is a Purpose

*The LORD has made everything
for his own purposes…*

Proverbs 16:4 NLT

When someone walks out of your life and you don't understand, it's easy to get discouraged. But when God brings it all together, when you meet the divine connection He has for you, somebody better than you ever dreamed, you'll look back and say that was a good day. Or what about the supervisor who tried to keep you down all those years? You didn't realize it at the time, but staying in that workplace with a good attitude, giving your best, and doing the right thing when the wrong thing was happening was developing your character, strengthening your spiritual muscles, getting you prepared for the next level. You wouldn't be who you are without that difficulty. You didn't like it at the time, but you look back now and say that was good.

Something Much Better

This plan of mine is not what you would work out, neither are my thoughts the same as yours!

Isaiah 55:8 TLB

Twice we tried to buy property for a new sanctuary, and both times the property was sold out from under us. We prayed about those properties and worked on the deals for months. I was so disappointed. I didn't see anything good about somebody's not keeping their word to sell us that property. It didn't make sense to me.

But I've learned that God's ways are better than our ways. When the former Compaq Center became available, I realized that the reason God closed those other doors is that He had something much better in store for us. God can see things that we can't see. Now I thank Him for closing those doors. I look back and know that was God keeping us from receiving less than He had in store for us.

Pushed Out, Pushed Up

If you are insulted because of the name of Christ, you are blessed, for the Spirit of glory and of God rests on you.

1 Peter 4:14

My father pastored a church for many years and gave his heart and soul to help the people. The church was growing, and his future was very bright. But when he started sharing how we're supposed to live a victorious, abundant life, it didn't fit into their denominational teaching, and he ended up having to leave the church. My mother had lifelong friends who never spoke to her again. My father and mother felt betrayed and discouraged.

But just as God opens doors, He closes doors. My parents went out and started Lakewood Church, and it grew into a church of thousands. Getting pushed out was one of the best things that could have happened to him. God knew that if my father stayed in that limited environment, he would never become who he was created to be.

Believe Big

Then Jesus said, "Did I not tell you that if you believe, you will see the glory of God?"

John 11:40

When you're hurting and disappointed, every thought tells you, "It's not fair, God. Why did You let this happen to me?" I'm asking you to trust Him. It may not seem good, but one day when God brings it all together, you'll look back and say, "It was a good Friday." I couldn't see it at the time when those two potential properties for a new sanctuary were sold out from under us, but it was good because it opened the door for us to get the Compaq Center.

Sometimes God closes doors because we're believing too small. You may have dreams that haven't worked out yet; you've had some disappointed Fridays. Don't get discouraged. God knows what He's doing. If you'll keep honoring Him, being your best, your Sunday is coming.

Resurrection

"He is not here; he has risen, just as he said. Come and see the place where he lay."

Matthew 28:6

You may be in a Friday right now— nothing seems good about your situation. You're dealing with an illness, or struggling in a relationship, or have people coming against you. It feels dark, lonely, discouraging. You don't see how it could ever work out. Stay in faith. God wouldn't have allowed it if it weren't going to move you forward. You're in Friday; the good news is that Sunday is coming, when you'll see your resurrection, so to speak. Sunday is when God vindicates you, heals you, promotes you, restores you. It's when He prepares a table for you in the presence of your enemies, when He pays you back double for that difficulty. That's what turns defeated Friday into good Friday. No more betrayed Friday, disappointed Friday. Now it's blessed Friday, joyful Friday, victorious Friday.

Things That Seem Bad

Commit your way to the LORD;
trust in him and he will do this.

Psalm 37:5

A couple went to the hospital every week to encourage the patients. One day the man was walking across the street to the hospital's main entrance when a speeding car came around the corner and hit him. They rushed him to the emergency room and discovered that he had bleeding in his brain. They took a full-body scan to see if anything else was injured and noticed a tumor on his kidney. When they did a biopsy, they found it was cancer. He had surgery to remove the kidney, and today he is cancer-free. The doctor told him that if they had not found that tumor, there was a good chance the cancer would have spread to other parts of his body and become life-threatening. It's all good—even things that at the time seem bad!

Behind the Scenes

And my God will meet all your needs according to the riches of his glory in Christ Jesus.

Philippians 4:19

Friend, it's all good—even getting hit by a car when you're doing a good deed as we saw in yesterday's reading. Most people would say, "Boy, that guy was unlucky." But God doesn't allow anything out of which He can't bring good. We don't always see it. "Joel, I've had a bunch of things happen to me that did nothing but pull me down." You don't know what God is doing behind the scenes. It may not have all come together yet. This is what faith is all about. When things happen that we don't like—disappointments, betrayals, bad breaks—we can get negative and live bitter. Or we can say, "God, I trust You. You know what's best for me. I believe that when it comes together, it's going to work for me and not against me."

16

Delays

"Isn't it clear that…GOD is sovereign, that he holds all things in his hand— every living soul, yes, every breathing creature?"

Job 12:10 MSG

Two young college students were traveling to Kenya to work on a mission project but missed their connecting flight in London due to heavy fog. They were disappointed and had to spend the night trying to sleep in the airport. About midway through the flight the next day, without warning the plane took a nosedive and started heading straight toward the ground. These young men heard noise in the cockpit that sounded like a struggle and found a deranged man had gotten into the cabin and overpowered the pilots. They grabbed that man, ripped him off the controls, and tied him up. Another minute or two, and everyone on that flight would have been killed. God held them back on purpose so they could save the plane and its passengers.

Ordered Steps

The steps of a good man are ordered by the Lord.

Psalm 37:23 NKJV

Sometimes God will inconvenience you in order to help somebody else. Instead of getting frustrated when our plans don't work out, we need to remember it's not all about us. "I don't like my job. The people are negative, they gossip, they compromise. When is God going to move me out?" Maybe God has you there on purpose to let your light shine and be a good influence on them. Quit fighting everything you don't like. If God has you there, He's ordered your steps. It may be uncomfortable, but instead of resisting it, trying to pray it away, why don't you embrace it? Say, "God, this is where You have me right now, so I'm going to be my best. I may not like it, it may feel bad, but I know a secret: it's all good."

January 18

Intended for Good

"You intended to harm me, but God intended it for good...the saving of many lives."

Genesis 50:20

After Joseph endured thirteen years of betrayals, disappointments, and lonely nights with a good attitude in an Egyptian prison, he was made the second-most powerful person in Egypt. Despite what he went through, he would have told you exactly what he later told his brothers who had sold him into slavery: it was all good. It was all a part of the plan.

Quit fighting everything you don't like. Quit being upset because you had a bad break, went through a disappointment, got a medical report that wasn't what you'd hoped for. God wouldn't allow it if it weren't going to work for your good. It looks like a setback, but really it's a setup to move you into your destiny. Just ask Joseph.

January 19

Fulfill His Purpose

*I cry out to God Most High, to God who
will fulfill his purpose for me.*

Psalm 57:2 NLT

I know a couple who initially struggled to
understand having a child born with special
needs, but now after starting a ministry
within their church to special needs children
and their parents, they would tell you it was
all good. You may not see it right now, but
there's a blessing in the darkness. When it
all comes together, it's going to work to your
advantage. It may be Friday in your life, with
no reason to call what you're going through
good, but don't worry, because Sunday is
coming. If you'll stay in faith, everything
that was meant to stop you, God is going to
use to push you forward. He's bringing it all
together right now. Good Friday is coming.
Blessed Friday, vindicated Friday, healthy
Friday, victorious Friday is headed your way!

JANUARY

20

Rely on Your God

If you are walking in darkness, without a ray of light, trust in the LORD and rely on your God.

Isaiah 50:10 NLT

When we think about what it means to be "blessed," most of the time we think of the good things that have happened to us. Perhaps our supervisor offered us a new position at work, or we may have overcome an illness and been blessed with a return to good health. Blessings and good times go hand in hand. It's easy have a grateful attitude when things are going our way.

But where are the blessings when we go through things we don't understand? The company was downsizing, and we were laid off. Somebody walked out of a relationship with us. It is possible to gain blessings in these difficult times of darkness that we cannot gain in the light…if we have the right attitude.

Seeds of Greatness

He will also send you rain for the seed you sow in the ground, and the food that comes from the land will be rich and plentiful.

Isaiah 30:23

All of us at some point will go through a dark place—a sickness, a divorce, a loss, a child who breaks our heart. It's easy to get discouraged, give up on our dreams, and think that's the end. But God uses the dark places. They're a part of His divine plan.

Think of a seed. As long as a seed remains in the light, it cannot germinate and will never become what it was created to be. The seed must be planted in the soil, in a dark place, so that the potential on the inside will come to life. In the same way, there are seeds of greatness in us—dreams, goals, talents, potential—that will only come to life in a dark place.

A Place of Preparation

"Moses was faithful as a servant in all God's house."

Hebrews 3:5

Throughout the Scripture, every person who did something great went through dark places. Moses made a mistake and killed an Egyptian man. He spent forty lonely years on the back side of the desert, feeling as though he had blown it. But in that dark place something was being shaped in his life. He was being prepared, developing patience, humility, strength, and trust. Without the dark place Moses would never have held up his rod and parted the Red Sea. He would never have led the Israelites out of slavery and toward the Promised Land.

The dark place was a prerequisite for his stepping into the fullness of his destiny, and it's a prerequisite for us as well.

Even in the Dark Places

The LORD said [to Elijah], "Go out and stand on the mountain in the presence of the LORD, for LORD is about to pass by."

1 Kings 19:11

Esther was an orphan, having lost both of her parents, and living in a foreign country. She felt alone, forsaken, abandoned, in a dark place. Yet God used her to help save the people of Israel. Joseph was betrayed by his own brothers, falsely accused of a crime, and put in prison, a dark place. But he ended up ruling a nation. Elijah descended from a great mountain victory into a dark place of depression so low that he wanted to die, yet he's one of the heroes of faith.

They didn't realize it at the time, but in that dark place they were being blessed. Something was happening on the inside.

Draw Near to God

*Let us draw near to God with a sincere heart and
with the full assurance that faith brings...*

Hebrews 10:22

A friend of mine was told that he was
going to lose his eyesight, but amazingly
he came out of surgery with his vision
perfectly fine. Now every morning he takes
time to gaze in wonder at his children and
give thanks.

You may not realize it, but it's in the dark
places where your character is developed,
where you learn to trust God and to
persevere, and where your spiritual muscles
are made strong. In the dark places you pray
more, you draw closer to God, and you take
time to get quiet and listen to what He's
saying. In the dark places you reevaluate your
priorities, you slow down and take time for
family, and you get a new appreciation for
what God has given you.

God's Approval

Am I now trying to win the approval of human beings, or of God?... If I were still trying to please people, I would not be a servant of Christ.

Galatians 1:10

One day a well-meaning person said to me, "Joel, I heard a guy talking negatively about you, and I was so sorry he said that." But I thought to myself, *You don't have to feel sorry for me. I buried my father. I saw my mother come through cancer. I learned how to minister when every voice told me I couldn't do it. I can handle somebody not liking me.*

When you go through enough dark places, you don't complain about life's little inconveniences. You don't get upset because you didn't get a parking spot or you got stuck in traffic. You don't get offended if a coworker was rude to you. You've been through too much to let that sour you. Your backbone has been made into steel.

JANUARY
26

Unshakable Confidence

I will be glad and rejoice in your love, for you saw my affliction and knew the anguish of my soul.

Psalm 31:7

When you go through a few dark places, it toughens you up. The dark places are what have made me into who I am today. I like the good times better. I prefer everything going my way, but it wasn't the good times that brought out the best in me. It was the lonely nights, the times I didn't think I could do it on my own, the times I didn't see a way—that's when I learned how to really pray, that's when I developed an unshakable confidence in God, that's when my faith was stretched.

Don't complain about the dark times; there's a blessing in the dark places. God is working something in your life that can only be worked in the fire of affliction.

Stretch and Grow

*For God is working in you,
giving you the desire
and the power to do
what pleases him.*

Philippians 2:13 NLT

When my father died and I was first
trying to learn how to minister, I was
so afraid to get up in front of people. There
were nights after dinner when I would go
to my closet to pray. Victoria would come
looking for me, asking the kids, "Where's
your dad?" She would find me in my closet
praying.

The truth is, I never prayed like that in
the good times. I didn't go out of my way
to draw closer to God when everything was
going my way. It was the dark places that
helped me to develop my spiritual muscles.
Even though I didn't like what I was going
through, being so uncomfortable forced me
to stretch and grow. I wouldn't change it for
anything. It's what makes us all better.

Iron in the Soul

*[Joseph] was laid in chains of iron and
his soul entered into the iron.*

Psalm 105:18 AMPC

When Joseph was falsely accused and put in prison for thirteen years, the Scripture says that his soul entered into the iron. In that prison Joseph developed strength, a perseverance that he could not have gotten any other way. There are some lessons you can only learn in the dark places.

Quit complaining about what you're going through, about how unfair it is, about who did you wrong. It may be uncomfortable, but it's working for your good. You're getting stronger; it's developing something in you that you can only get in the dark. You can't reach your highest potential being in the light all the time. To have no opposition, no problems, and nobody coming against you may sound good, but it will stunt your growth.

January 29

Enlarged

*Out of my distress I called upon the Lord;
the Lord answered me and set me free
and in a large place.*

Psalm 118:5 AMPC

King David didn't get enlarged in the good times; he was enlarged when things weren't going his way. While he was alone out in the shepherds' fields, it looked as though he would never accomplish his dreams. But those years helped prepare him to become a champion. When he killed Goliath, it happened because he went through the dark places with a good attitude. When he wasn't getting his way and he felt as though God had forgotten about him, he just kept doing the right thing. His attitude was, *God, this is a dark place, but I'm developing patience and perseverance and learning to trust You.* At the right time he came out of that dark place increased, promoted, and better off than he had been before.

JANUARY

30

Through the Darkest Valley

Even though I walk through the darkest valley, I will fear no evil, for you are with me; your rod and your staff, they comfort me.

Psalm 23:4

It's not a coincidence that David says, in effect, "The same God who leads me to the green pastures and the still waters is the same God who will lead me through the valley of the shadow of death."

We can all trust God when we're resting in the green pastures and beside the still waters—that's easy. But He is asking you to trust Him when you're in the dark valley. You may feel alone, abandoned, and mistreated, but God is still leading you. It may not be easy, but faith is trusting in God when life doesn't make sense. Dare to believe that He's blessing you even in the dark places. Believe that what's meant for your harm is going to work to your advantage.

Overflow

You prepare a table before me in the presence of my enemies. You anoint my head with oil; my cup overflows.

Psalm 23:5

David says that *after* you go through the dark valley, God will prepare a table before you in the presence of your enemies. You have to go through the loneliness, through the sickness, through the betrayal before you get that fresh anointing, that new beginning. You have to go through the job where you're not being treated right, through the struggle, the lack, the debt, before you make it to where your cup runs over.

Too often we want the overflow but not the valley. In the dark places is where we prove to God what we're really made of. Can God trust you with more of His favor, with greater influence and more resources? You have to be faithful in the shepherds' field, where you're not getting your way.

New Beginnings

"Forget the former things; do not dwell on the past. See, I am doing a new thing!... I am making a way in the wilderness and streams in the wasteland."

Isaiah 43:18–19

FEBRUARY 1

When my father went to be with the Lord in 1999, that was the greatest challenge I had ever faced—a dark place. When you go through a loss, it's easy to get discouraged and feel as though God let you down and there will never be any more good days. But I've learned that every time something dies in my life, something else is coming to life. It looks like an end, but God has a new beginning. You lost a job or a major client, but God has new opportunities and new levels for you. If you'll go through the valley trusting, believing, knowing that God is in control, you'll come to the table prepared for you, into the fresh anointing, and increase to where your cup is running over.

Amazed with His Goodness

*I remain confident of this:
I will see the goodness
of the LORD in the land
of the living.*

Psalm 27:13

You may have a lot of questions about why certain things have happened in your life. Think about this: an exclamation point is simply a question mark straightened out. If you want God to turn your question marks, the things you don't understand, into exclamation points, you have to trust Him. Instead of wondering why something happened, dare to say, "God, I know You're still on the throne. I may not understand this valley I'm in, but I know that on the other side is my exclamation point. The table is already prepared, a fresh anointing is coming with increase, promotion, and a new level." If you go through the dark places like that, you'll see that question mark turned into an exclamation point. God will amaze you with His goodness.

The Exclamation Point

*The LORD blessed the latter part of Job's life
more than the former part.*

Job 42:12

You may be in a dark place right now. You went through a breakup, and you're hurt, lonely, wondering if you'll ever be happy again. I can tell you firsthand that if you keep moving forward, honoring God, He'll bring somebody into your life who is better than you ever imagined. The latter part of your life will be better than the first part. God has an exclamation point waiting for you.

Maybe you're dealing with a serious illness. Stay in faith—the exclamation point is coming. My mother was diagnosed with terminal cancer, and thirty-eight years later, she's still healthy and strong. That's good, but here's the exclamation point. Every week she goes to the hospital to pray for other sick people. That's God making the enemy pay.

Unstoppable

"The One who breaks open the way will go up before them; they will break through the gate and go out...the LORD at their head."

Micah 2:13

Perhaps you're in a dark place in your finances. You had a setback or lost a client, and you're wondering, *Is it ever going to get better?* Yes, on the other side of that valley you're going to find your cup that runs over—increase, abundance, a new level of your destiny. You may have been in that valley for a long time, but you're about to see the breakthrough. Don't stop believing. Get your fire back, because God did not bring you this far to leave you.

People don't determine your destiny, but God does. Bad breaks can't stop you. God has the final say. If you'll go through the dark places with a good attitude and keep doing the right thing, you will see the goodness of God.

Blessed in the Breaking

Taking the five loaves and the two fish and looking up to heaven, [Jesus] gave thanks and broke the loaves.

Matthew 14:19

When Jesus was about to feed a multitude of thousands of people, "He broke the loaves," and the bread was multiplied. Notice the blessing was in the breaking. The more He broke it, the more it multiplied.

There are times in life when we feel broken: we have broken dreams, a broken heart. When you feel broken, don't get bitter, don't give up on your dreams. That brokenness is not the end; it's a sign that God is about to multiply. That brokenness may have been meant to stop you, but if you'll stay in faith, God is going to use it to increase you. The hurt you feel is real, but the truth is that it is setting you up for God to increase you.

On the Other Side

They all ate and were satisfied, and the disciples picked up twelve basketfuls of broken pieces that were left over.

Matthew 14:20

Jesus took a little boy's lunch, and as He broke the loaves they multiplied and fed a tremendous multitude and had basketfuls of leftovers.

If you have gone through more than your share of bad breaks, take heart. The more broken you are, the more God is going to increase you. The bigger the disappointment, the bigger the blessing. The more they hurt you, the more He's going to reward you. The brokenness is only temporary. Don't settle in the valley, don't even get comfortable in the valley, for the valley is not your home. The Shepherd is leading you through the valley. On the other side is abundance, fullness of joy, great relationships, health and wholeness, and dreams coming to pass.

Unleashed Potential

*"He took one of the seedlings of the land
and put it in fertile soil.…and it sprouted
and became a low, spreading vine."*

Ezekiel 17:5-6

You can have a seed on your desk for a lifetime, but it will never become what it was created to be until you put plant it in the ground. As long as it's on the desk where it's comfortable, the seed's potential will stay locked up on the inside. Only after it's planted and goes through the process of germination—when the outer shell breaks off and the new growth begins—will it blossom and bring forth much fruit. The problem with many people is that they want the fruit, but they don't want to go through the process. They don't want to have to stretch or deal with adversity, opposition, or betrayal. But without the dark place, your potential will stay locked on the inside.

Planted, Not Buried

"Unless a kernel of wheat is planted in the soil and dies, it remains alone. But its death will produce many new kernels."

John 12:24 NLT

If you were to ask a seed that's about to be planted, I'm sure it would say, "I don't want to go into the dirt. It's dark, it's lonely, and it's uncomfortable." The seed feels as though it's been buried, as though it's the end, but what the seed doesn't realize is that it's not buried; it's planted. It has the life of Almighty God on the inside. That dark place is a critical part of the process. Once it germinates and grows, instead of being one little buried seed, it ends up being a beautiful flower, blossoming and bearing much fruit. If you were to ask the flower when it was fully in blossom, it would say, "I didn't like the dark place, but I realize now it was a blessing. Look what it brought out of me. Look what I've become!"

New, New, New

*This means that anyone
who belongs to Christ has
become a new person. The
old life is gone; a new
life has begun!*

2 Corinthians 5:17 NLT

There will be times in life when it feels as
though you're buried, and thoughts will
tell you, *You've seen your best days. That layoff
ruined your career. That divorce tainted your
future.* Have a new perspective. You're not
buried; you're planted. If you never went
through the dark place—the loneliness, the
disappointment, the loss—you would never
discover what's on the inside. Your potential
is about to be released. You're going to come
out better, stronger, fully in blossom, and
bearing much fruit. When you feel as if
something is dying, it's dark, you feel the
pressure of the dirt, you don't see a way out,
that's a sign that something new is about to
come to life—new growth, new talent, new
opportunities.

Much Fruit

"The seed that fell on good soil represents those who truly hear and understand God's word and produce a harvest of thirty, sixty, or even a hundred times..."

Matthew 13:23 NLT

When my father went to be with the Lord, I felt as though I were buried. But in that dark time, when something was dying, God was birthing something new. That's when I discovered gifts and talents that I hadn't known I had. I didn't like the process, but that's what caused me to blossom.

In dark places like that you have to remind yourself that even though it feels as if something is dying, something else is coming to life. You're not buried; you're planted. When you come out, you're going to bear much fruit. My challenge is for you to be willing to go through the process. Don't fight the dark places. It's there to bring out the greatness on the inside.

Night Seasons

And let us not grow weary while doing good, for in due season we shall reap if we do not lose heart.

Galatians 6:9 NKJV

There are times in all our lives when we're praying and believing, but we don't see anything changing. We're still dealing with the same problem. We can feel alone, forgotten, as though our situation is never going to change. It's a night season. We can't see what God is doing, but God is working behind the scenes. He does His greatest work in the dark.

In the dark times, you have to remind yourself that God is still in control. Just because you don't see anything happening doesn't mean that God is not working. He doesn't always show you what He's up to. You have to learn to trust Him in the night seasons when things aren't going your way and you don't see anything happening.

Dare to Trust Him

When my spirit was overwhelmed and weak within me [wrapped in darkness], You knew my path.

Psalm 142:3 AMP

FEBRUARY 12

As a young man, David defeated Goliath. It was a great victory. But after that he spent years running from King Saul, hiding in caves, sleeping in the desert. I'm sure he prayed, "God, deliver me from Saul. This is not right." But it was as though the heavens were silent. God didn't change it. It was a night season—a time of testing, a time of proving. We can either choose to get negative and live discouraged, or we can choose to say, "God, I don't understand it, but I trust in You. I know You're not just the God of the daytime, but also the God of the night seasons."

You may not see anything happening, but God is at work. Dare to trust Him. Keep moving forward in faith, keep believing.

Joy Comes in the Morning

Weeping may endure for a night,
but joy comes in the morning.

Psalm 30:5 NKJV

In the Scripture, Ruth lost her husband at an early age. She was devastated, heartbroken. She could have given up on life and lived in self-pity. But she understood this principle: the night seasons are not the end. Ruth went on to meet another man. They fell in love, got married, and had a baby. Her story didn't end in the dark.

When things aren't working out and you feel as though you're going in the wrong direction, don't get discouraged because God has not changed it yet. Your story doesn't end in the night. The bad breaks, the disappointments, the losses, and the sicknesses are simply additional steps on the way to your destiny. It's just a matter of time before the morning breaks forth.

The Rain Falls on All

There lived in the land of Uz a man named Job—a good man who feared God and stayed away from evil.

Job 1:1 TLB

Like other Old Testament heroes of the faith, Job went through a night season. He was happy, healthy, and successful, but out of nowhere he came down with a very painful illness. He lost his business, and he lost his sons and daughters. His whole world was turned upside down. What's interesting is that Job loved God. He was a person of excellence and integrity. All that happened to him would make more sense if he were a person who was not honoring God.

But the Scripture says, "God sends the rain on the just and the unjust." Just because you're a good person doesn't mean you're not going to have some night seasons. It means that you're getting some rain. Without the rain you couldn't grow.

Don't Magnify the Difficulty

"I, too, have been assigned months of futility, long and weary nights of misery."

Job 7:3 NLT

J ob did what many of us do in the difficult times, the serious and heartbreaking times. He focused on the problem, magnified what was wrong, and let it overwhelm him. Job was saying, "This is how my story ends. I will never again experience pleasure. I've been assigned to nights of misery." The mistake he made was thinking it was permanent.

What you're going through may be difficult, but the good news is that you are going through it. It's not your final destination. It's a night season, not a night lifetime. God wouldn't have allowed it if it were going to keep you from your destiny. He has you in the palms of His hands. He already has the solution, and the breakthrough is headed your way.

Laugh Again

"He will yet fill your mouth with laughter and your lips with shouts of joy."

Job 8:21

In Job's darkest hour, when he was the most discouraged, God said through one of Job's friends, "Job, it looks bad. You don't understand it, but don't worry. It's not permanent. It's just a season. I'm about to fill your mouth with laughter."

God is saying to you what He said to Job. Life may not have been fair, but you're not going to live discouraged, overwhelmed by problems, or burdened down by illnesses. Joy is coming. Health is coming. Breakthroughs are coming. Promotion is coming. God is about to fill your mouth with laughter. That means God's going to do something so unusual, so extraordinary, that you'll be so amazed that all you can do is laugh. Your mourning is going to be turned to dancing.

Great Days Ahead

After this, Job lived a hundred and forty years;
he saw his children and their children to the
fourth generation. And so Job died,
an old man and full of years.

Job 42:16–17

Job not only made it through the night season, but God restored double what he'd lost. He came out with twice the oxen, sheep, camels, and donkeys. He felt twice as healthy. God always makes the enemy pay for bringing trouble. If you'll stay in faith, you won't just come out, you will come out better than you were before.

When we think of Job, we usually think of all his suffering. The truth is, that was just one season. You may be in a dark time, but, like Job, you're going to come through it and still live a long, blessed life. It says, "After this, Job lived 140 years." After the night season, after the disappointment or loss, there are still many great days ahead.

February 18

After

*"But as for you, be strong and do not give up,
for your work will be rewarded."*

2 Chronicles 15:7

My father went through a night season. He was married at a very young age. Unfortunately, the marriage didn't work out. He was devastated when it failed, resigned from his church, and was told he would never pastor again. The good news is, people don't determine your destiny; God does. Two years later, he got back into the ministry, and he later married my mother. They had five children and were married for almost fifty years. They started Lakewood and pastored for forty years, touching the world. This all happened *after* the night season. He went on to live a long, blessed, faith-filled life.

Don't let the night seasons convince you that you've seen your best days. You wouldn't be alive unless God had something amazing in front of you.

All Is Well

19

"...say to her, 'Is all well with you? Is all well with your husband? Is all well with the child?'" And she answered, "All is well."

2 Kings 4:26 ESV

In the dark times, it's easy to talk about the difficulties and exaggerate our problems. All that's going to do is make you more discouraged and take your joy. Instead of complaining, one of the best things you can say is, "All is well." When you say, "All is well," what you're really saying is, "God is still on the throne, and I'm not going to live upset, bitter, and guilty. This night season will pass." Somebody may say, "Well, I thought the medical report wasn't good." And you respond, "Yes, that's true, but all is well. God is restoring health back to me."

Every day that you stay in faith and keep a good attitude despite the darkness, you're passing the test. That night season will pass.

Light Comes Bursting In

*When darkness overtakes
[the righteous], light will
come bursting in.*

Psalm 112:4 TLB

After yesterday's reading, perhaps you were
wondering, *How can I say "All is well"
when I lost a loved one or lost my job?* You can
say it because you know the night season is
temporary. You know joy is coming. It's going
to happen suddenly, unexpectedly; you won't
see it coming. You woke up, and it was still
dark. Nothing had changed, but suddenly
you get the break you need. Suddenly your
health turns around. Suddenly you meet the
right person. The light comes bursting in.

Now, don't talk yourself into being
miserable. Keep a report of victory coming
out of your mouth. If you're going to
magnify something, don't magnify your
problems; magnify your God. Talk about
His greatness, talk about His favor. God is
saying, "All is well."

Come Up Higher

Moses was a very humble man, more humble than anyone else on the face of the earth.

Numbers 12:3

In the reading for January 22, we saw that Moses made a mistake that put him into a night season. Forty years after Moses' mistake, God said, "All right, Moses, now you're ready for Me to use you to deliver My people." In that desert place, Moses had learned to wait on God, to listen to His voice, to walk in humility. He came up higher in his character.

Whatever God started in your life, He's going to finish. He's already taken into account every wrong turn and mistake in your life. It may feel like the end to you, but the truth is, it's a time of testing, a time of proving, when your character is being developed. God is getting you prepared for where He's taking you.

Pass the Tests

For you, God, tested us;
you refined us like silver.

Psalm 66:10

You have to be prepared for where God is taking you. Moses couldn't handle it the first time. He made a mistake and had to run, but God didn't write him off. He used the night season to refine him. In the difficult times, we have to stay pliable, stay open, and say, "God, make me and mold me. Show me where I need to change." You grow in the tough times.

In the night seasons, you need to pass the tests, change where you need to change, and deal with the areas that God is bringing to light. Then, as He did for Moses, because your character has been developed, God will bring you out of that night season and get you to where you're supposed to be.

Do the Right Thing

*"But the LORD forbid that I should lay
a hand on the LORD's anointed."*

1 Samuel 26:11

When Saul was chasing David through the desert, there were several opportunities for David to kill Saul. He could have taken Saul's life and gotten rid of his problem, so to speak. But David wouldn't do it. He knew that Saul had been anointed by God. After he passed these tests, after David showed God that he was a man of character, integrity, and forgiveness, God took care of Saul and David was made the king.

In the night seasons, you need to prove to God that you'll do the right thing when it's hard, and you'll forgive others even though they hurt you. We can only develop some things in the dark. Without the night seasons, we wouldn't become all God created us to be.

Transformation

*Do not conform to the pattern of
this world, but be transformed by the
renewing of your mind.*

Romans 12:2

A caterpillar can be going along just fine,
but down deep something says, "You
were made to fly." He gets excited, thinking,
Yes, that's right! Then he looks in the mirror
and says, "That's impossible. I'm just a
glorified worm." But one day the caterpillar
spins a cocoon around itself. It's dark. He
can't move or eat. If you were to talk to
him, he'd say, "Let me go back to being a
caterpillar. I'm uncomfortable. It's dark. It's
lonely." What he doesn't realize is that in
the dark, a transformation is taking place.
Before long he starts feeling some wings,
then he gets the strength to push out of that
cocoon. Then, instead of crawling on the
ground, he's a beautiful butterfly floating
through the air.

FEBRUARY

25

Higher Things

And we all, who with unveiled faces contemplate the Lord's glory, are being transformed into his image with ever-increasing glory.

2 Corinthians 3:18

There are night seasons when God incubates us like He does a caterpillar in a cocoon. In the dark places a transformation is taking place. You're growing, you're being refined, so keep reminding yourself that your wings are developing. You're about to step up to a new level. No more crawling, living in mediocrity. You were made for higher things.

You may be in a night season, but by faith I can see a wing coming out of your cocoon. This is no time to be discouraged; you're on the verge of becoming a beautiful butterfly and taking off in flight. You're about to go places that you've never dreamed of. Keep a good attitude; it's all a part of the process. God is changing you from glory to glory.

In the Desert Places

FEBRUARY

26

When Jacob awoke from his sleep, he thought, "Surely the LORD is in this place, and I was not aware of it."

Genesis 28:16

Jacob was a deceiver. You would think that God wouldn't have anything to do with him. But God keeps working with us and showing us His mercy. One night while Jacob was on a long journey through the desert and in a hard place, I'm sure he thought that God had forgotten about him. While he was sleeping, he had a dream in which he saw the Lord standing at the top of a huge staircase and saying, "Jacob, I will protect you wherever you go. I will be with you continually until I give you everything that I have promised." When Jacob woke up, he was in awe. What's interesting is that Jacob was in the desert. God was showing us that He's the God of hard places, of lonely times, of night seasons.

February 27

Wherever You Go

"I am with you and will watch over you wherever you go…I will not leave you until I have done what I have promised you."

Genesis 28:15

Similar to Jacob in yesterday's reading, you may be in a difficult place now. Perhaps you're fighting a battle in your health, dealing with depression, or raising a special needs child. You feel alone, forgotten, and discouraged. God is right there with you, and, as they did for Jacob, I believe the heavens are about to open up. God is going to make things happen that you couldn't make happen. Your health is going to improve. You're going to break that addiction. The right people are going to show up. You're going to join Jacob and say, "The Lord is in this place! The Lord healed me from cancer." "The Lord freed me from depression." "The Lord blessed my business." He's not going to stop until He's given you everything that He's promised.

February 28

Night Shifts

*Indeed, he who watches over Israel
will neither slumber nor sleep.*

Psalm 121:4

You've heard the phrase *the night shift*. It refers to people who work during the night. But think of it another way. In the night, things are going to shift. The Scripture says, "God never sleeps." He doesn't just work the night shift, He shifts things in the night. You may be in a night season, and you may not see how the difficulties you face can work out. Don't worry—God specializes in shifting things in the dark. The God who works the night shift is going to shift things in your favor. There's going to be a shift in your health, a shift in your finances, a shift with that addiction. You think you're going to have it for years. It looks permanent. No, get ready for a night shift.

At Midnight

About midnight Paul and Silas were praying and singing hymns to God… Suddenly there was such a violent earthquake that… everyone's chains came loose.

Acts 16:25–26

Paul and Silas had been spreading the good news in the city of Philippi, for which they had been beaten with rods and held in the prison dungeon. But at midnight, as they were singing praises to God, suddenly there was a great earthquake. The prison doors flung open, and the chains came off their feet. They walked out as free men. When did it happen? At midnight. It was just another night shift for the God who works the night shift.

Things may look permanent in your life—the addiction, the sickness, the panic attacks, the lack and struggle. Thoughts will tell you, *You'll always have to deal with that.* Don't believe those lies. You're in a night season, which means you're in perfect position for a night shift.

While You Sleep

So the LORD God caused the man to fall into a deep sleep; and while he was sleeping, he took one of the man's ribs…

Genesis 2:21

Adam was all by himself in the Garden of Eden. Life was good. He was naming the animals, enjoying the crystal-clear river, the beautiful trees, the delicious fruit. There were no problems. Adam didn't think it could get any better. But God didn't want him to live alone, so He put him in a night season, took a rib from his side, and used it to create a woman. When Adam woke up and saw Eve, I can imagine the first thing he said was, "Wow, God, You've outdone Yourself!" But I'm sure that he hadn't understood why God was putting him to sleep when life had seemed perfect. If God didn't put us to sleep, so to speak, we would never see the fullness of what He has in store for us.

When You Awake

The grace of our Lord [His amazing, unmerited favor and blessing] flowed out in superabundance [for me...].

1 Timothy 1:14 AMP

God put Adam into a deep sleep, and you may feel as though God has put you to sleep. Things have slowed down. You're in a challenging situation. Be encouraged because the dark places are leading you to the amazing things God has in store. You may not understand it, but God wouldn't have allowed it if He weren't going to use it to your advantage. Right now, God is working behind the scenes. He sees what you're dealing with and knows how you feel. When you wake up and see what God has been up to, the first thing you're going to say is, "Wow, God, I never dreamed You'd take me here!" "I never dreamed I'd be this healthy again!" Get ready because God has some *wows* in your future.

Secret Frustrations

"Do not be dismayed, for I am your God. I will strengthen you and help you; I will uphold you with my righteous right hand."

Isaiah 41:10 TLB

MARCH 3

All of us have secret frustrations—things that we know God could change. We know He could open the door, or remove the temptation, or give us the healing, but it's not happening. It's easy to get stuck with the "why" questions.

We have to realize that God is sovereign. We're not going to understand why everything happens or doesn't happen. God doesn't remove some things. He waits a long time to change some situations. You have to trust that He knows what's best for you. If you keep the right attitude, all those frustrating situations that are not changing won't work against you, but instead will work for you. Don't let the contradictions of life cause you to get sour and give up on your dreams.

Tap into Grace

But he said to me, "My grace is sufficient for you,
for my power is made perfect in weakness."

2 Corinthians 12:9

The apostle Paul talked about his secret frustration, which he called "a thorn in the flesh." Scholars have debated whether it was a physical condition such as an illness or something else. Whatever was bothering him, Paul prayed three times for God to remove it. One translation of the Scripture says he "implored" God to take it away. That means that Paul gave it his best argument. "God, I've served You. I've been my best. I've prayed for others, and they've been healed. God, please take it away." But what's interesting is that God never removed that thorn. Rather, God's answer to him was, "Paul, tap into My grace. It's sufficient for you. You are well able to enjoy your life in spite of this secret frustration."

If It Never Changes

Though…there are no grapes on the vines…
yet I will rejoice in the LORD, I will be
joyful in God my Savior.

Habakkuk 3:17–18

Is there something you've implored God to change, perhaps a situation in your health, your finances, a relationship? You've asked again and again, but nothing's improved. I'm not saying to give up and settle there in a dark place. What I'm saying is that if God is not removing it or changing it, don't let it steal your joy. God has given you the grace to be there. The right attitude is, *I'm not going to let this frustrate me anymore. God, I know Your grace is sufficient for me. I have the power to be here with a good attitude. I believe that at the right time You will change it; but if it never changes, I'm still going to be my best and honor You.*

MARCH 6

Don't Get Stuck

Yet you, LORD, are our Father.
We are the clay, you are
the potter; we are all the
work of your hand.

Isaiah 64:8

When you have a secret frustration, don't focus on it. When we keep asking why God hasn't changed something, we get stuck on the whys of life and can't fulfill our destiny. Faith is trusting God when life doesn't make sense.

If you're going to reach your full potential, you can't be a weakling. You have to be a warrior. There will be things you don't understand, but God knows what He's doing. His ways are better than our ways. His thoughts are higher than our thoughts. He is the Potter, and we are the clay. If it's supposed to be removed, He'll remove it. If not, dig your heels in and fight the good fight of faith. You have the grace you need for every situation.

Reminders of Grace

Jesus said to him, "Rise, take up your bed and walk."

John 5:8 NKJV

When Jesus healed a man who had been crippled for thirty-eight years, He told him to take his bed with him even though he didn't need it anymore. But Jesus was saying, "Take the thing that held you back for years with you as a reminder of what I've done in your life." It was a seeming contradiction. I can imagine him helping somebody else who was struggling. They would say, "How can you help me? You're still carrying around that thing that held you back." The man said, "This is not a limitation to slow me down. It's a testimony of what God has done in my life. It reminds me to give God praise. It reminds me of the dark place He brought me from, and that if He did it for me once, He'll do it for me again."

March 8

Strength in Weakness

For when I am weak, then I am strong.

2 Corinthians 12:10

When I first started ministering, I was insecure and intimidated and felt unqualified. Over the years I've gotten more confident and come to better understand who I am. But when I get up to speak, I still feel some of the past limitations and weaknesses. However, I see them in a new light. They don't intimidate me now; rather, they remind me of my dependency on God.

What I'm saying is that even though God frees you from certain things, you may still have your bed like the healed man in yesterday's reading. The weakness, the limitation, may not totally go away. God wants it to be a reminder to you of where you came from. That bed is not there to discourage you but to inspire you.

No Boasting

The LORD said to Gideon, "The people with you are too many…lest Israel boast over me, saying, 'My own hand has saved me.'"

Judges 7:2 ESV

When I first started ministering and felt so insecure, God didn't make me into a different person. The reason He doesn't always remove all your weaknesses is that you would end up thinking you can do it on your own and thinking you have it all figured out, and you'd end up right back where you were. But if you'll see your weakness, your temptation, as a reminder to ask God for His help and to thank Him for what He's done, you'll continue to move forward in spite of what's come against you. I can say now, "Yes, I have my weaknesses, but I'm pastoring the church. I have my limitations, but I'm helping other people. I have my temptations, but I'm enjoying life, and I'm healthy and whole and blessed."

He Knows What You Need

"Master, please, I don't talk well. I've never been good with words, neither before nor after you spoke to me. I stutter and stammer."

Exodus 4:10 MSG

When God told Moses to go tell Pharaoh to let the people of Israel go, Moses was insecure and didn't feel qualified. However, God showed Moses miraculous signs so that he would go into the courts of Pharaoh with confidence, knowing that God was with him.

But Moses had another concern. He said, "God, I can't stand before Pharaoh because I have a speech problem." You would have thought, since God just did all those miracles, He would simply touch Moses' tongue and take away the stuttering. But God didn't remove that problem. God was saying to Moses what He said to Paul: "My strength is made perfect in your weakness. If I needed to remove it for you to fulfill your destiny, I would have removed it."

Come Back to Peace

You will keep in perfect peace those whose minds are steadfast, because they trust in you.

Isaiah 26:3

Are you waiting for God to remove a secret frustration or weakness before you can be happy, before you can pursue a dream, finish school, or be good to somebody? You have what you need. If God is not removing it, it's not an accident. If He's not changing what you want changed, there is a reason. You may not be able to see it, it may not make sense to you, but you have to trust Him. God has your best interests at heart.

You're not supposed to live frustrated because a problem isn't turning around. Don't live stressed out because a family member is not doing right or be upset because a dream is taking too long. Come back to the place of peace.

Seeming Contradictions

We have this treasure in earthen vessels, that the excellence of the power may be of God and not of us.

2 Corinthians 4:7 NKJV

The Scripture talks about how we have treasure "in earthen vessels." Yet all of us have imperfections within our clay pot—seeming contradictions. There's something that's not being removed or changed that could easily irritate us and cause us to live frustrated. What is it for you? Perhaps you say, "If I didn't have this back pain or this weight problem, I would be happy." It might be a coworker who gets on your nerves. For many people, it's the hurts from going through a bad childhood, then a divorce.

Whatever it is, God is saying to you, "My grace is sufficient. Quit fighting it. Quit letting it steal your joy. When I am ready to remove it, I will; but until then, tap into My grace. Trust Me."

Only God Knows

*And lest I should be
exalted above measure
by the abundance of the
revelations, a thorn in the
flesh was given to me...*

2 Corinthians 12:7 NKJV

MARCH 13

I f God is not removing a frustration in your
life, there's a reason. Nothing happens by
accident. Paul thought the thorn in his flesh
was to keep him from getting proud, to keep
him from getting puffed up because of the
great revelations he had been given. Only
God knows the reason He allows thorns to
remain in our lives. That secret frustration
may just be for a time of testing. It may be
for a time when you have to prove to God
that you're going to be content and do your
best when things are not going your way.
You're going to keep giving even when you're
not receiving. You're going to keep trying
when every door is closing. You're going to
keep doing the right thing even when you're
not seeing right results.

Developing Character

"Behold, I have refined you, but not as silver;
I have tested you in the furnace of affliction."

Isaiah 48:10 NKJV

There are some things you can only learn in the trial of affliction. You can't learn them by reading a book or listening to a message. You have to experience them. That place of testing is where your spiritual muscles are developed. You can't get stronger without exercising those muscles during times of intense pressure. That's not easy. But if we stay with it, it will work for us, not against us. We will be growing, getting stronger, being prepared for new levels.

Your gifts may take you to a certain level, but if you don't have the character to match them, you won't stay there. Character is developed in the tough times, when you're not getting your way but you keep doing the right thing.

Prepared for Promotion

If you keep yourself pure, you will be…ready for the Master to use you for every good work.

2 Timothy 2:21 NLT

As Paul did, we've all asked, "God, please remove this secret frustration." "Remove this person at work who gets on my nerves." "Make my spouse more loving." "Give us the baby we've been praying for." Until God changes it, if you'll keep doing the right thing, not letting it sour you, then here's the beauty of it: even if the situation never changes, you will change. You're getting stronger, you're coming up higher, you're being prepared for the fullness of your destiny.

You can't be promoted without preparation. God won't give you a hundred-pound blessing when He knows you can lift only fifty pounds. If He gave you the hundred pounds, it wouldn't be a blessing; it would be a burden. He has to get you prepared.

Stay in Faith

16

*"Look, I go forward, but…
I cannot see Him. But He
knows the way that I take;
when He has tested me,
I shall come forth as gold."*

Job 23:8–10 NKJV

I've learned that our character is more important than our talent. We can have all the talent in the world, but if we don't have strong character, we won't go very far. We can all trust God in the good times. But can you trust Him with the secret frustrations that haven't changed? You've prayed and believed, but God hasn't removed it. The question is not only if you can trust God but, more important, if God can trust you. Will you pass that test and stay in faith even when you don't understand it? If you'll trust God, you will not only enjoy your life more, but He will remove everything that's supposed to be removed, and you will rise higher, overcome obstacles, and become everything you were created to be.

Character First

[Put first things first.]
Prepare your work outside
and get it ready for yourself
in the field; and afterward
build your house.

Proverbs 24:27 AMPC

For a period of time, my father held big crusades in other countries with crowds of fifty thousand people and saw God do amazing things. But when he returned to pastor Lakewood, instead of speaking to huge crowds, he was speaking to ninety people, three times a week, year after year. Down deep my father had this secret frustration. "God, I'm honoring You, but the church is not growing."

What he didn't realize was that he was changing. He was developing character; he was proving to God that he would be faithful in the tough times. Then, in 1972, people started pouring in from all parts of the city. Lakewood grew and grew to a church of thousands. God had used the dark place to bring my father into abundant blessing.

March 18

Be Your Best

*Do your best to present yourself to God
as one approved, a worker who does
not need to be ashamed...*

2 Timothy 2:15

Maybe you're doing the right thing, but your secret frustration is not changing—you're not seeing any growth, you're not being promoted. Nothing may be happening on the outside, but if you keep the right attitude, something is happening on the inside. God is changing you.

Keep doing the right thing, keep being good to people, keep giving it your best and having an excellent spirit. God is growing you up. You're being prepared for promotion. Too many people let these secret frustrations cause them to get sour, lose their passion, and slack off. Recognize that what you're facing is a test. If you'll keep doing the right thing, God will get you to where you're supposed to be.

March 19

The Right Attitude

When Rachel saw that she bore Jacob no children, Rachel envied her sister, and said to Jacob, "Give me children, or else I die!"

Genesis 30:1 NKJV

In Genesis 29–30 is the story of two sisters named Rachel and Leah, who both became wives of a young man named Jacob. The Scripture says, "Rachel was beautiful in every way, with a lovely face and shapely figure" and that Jacob adored her. I'm sure that people who saw her thought that she was one blessed lady. But Rachel's dream was to have a baby, and she was barren and stuck in a really dark place.

The point is, everybody is dealing with a secret frustration. Rachel, who was blessed with great looks and a loving husband, had one crucial matter she didn't understand, one thing God was not removing. Her attitude had to become, *God, if it never changes, if I never have children, I'm still going to be happy.*

Be at Peace

*[Jacob] loved Rachel
more than Leah.*

Genesis 29:30 NKJV

While Leah in yesterday's reading had none of Rachel's outward beauty, she gave Jacob one son after another, six strong, handsome boys as well as one beautiful daughter. Life seemed good for Leah, and God had blessed her with a healthy family. However, Leah too had a secret frustration, a dark place. While her children brought so much joy to her life, I can hear her saying every night, "God, this is so painful. Why doesn't Jacob love me more? Why don't You change his heart?"

Leah's attitude had to become, *God, if my marriage never improves, I'm not going to live sour. If somebody looks better than I, has more than I, is more talented than I, I'm not going to be jealous or bitter. I'm at peace with who I am.*

At the Right Time

Then God remembered Rachel's plight and answered her prayers by enabling her to have children.

Genesis 30:22 NLT

I n the past two readings we considered the two sisters, Rachel and Leah. Whether you're like Rachel, blessed in one area, or like Leah, blessed in another, there will be things that frustrate you. But when you live in peace, you won't be trying to figure out why someone else got the looks or someone else has all the children, or be trying to get your husband to love you more. You give it to God. At the right time God will remove what's supposed to be removed. He'll change what's supposed to be changed.

That's what happened with Rachel. Years later God removed the barrenness, and she had a remarkable son named Joseph. The darkness gave way to the light, and that secret frustration gave way to a huge blessing.

A Made-up Mind

Oh, give thanks to the LORD, for He is good! For His mercy endures forever.

Psalm 107:1 NKJV

For most of my father's life, he struggled with high blood pressure. He was changing lives all over the world, yet God never took this sickness away. But he had a made-up mind. His attitude was, *God, I'm going to be my best whether or not You heal me.*

After my father had to go on dialysis, one night he couldn't sleep, and my brother-in-law Gary was with him. Gary asked my father what he thought about the difficulty he was going through. My father said, "I don't understand it all, but I know this: His mercy endures forever." A few seconds later he had a heart attack and went to be with the Lord. Whatever secret frustration you're dealing with, make the decision that he made: if it never changes, you're still going to stay in faith.

Even If He Doesn't

"But even if he does not, we want you to know, Your Majesty, that we will not serve your gods."

Daniel 3:18

MARCH 23

This is what three Hebrew teenagers did in the Scripture. They wouldn't bow down to the king of Babylon's golden idol. He was so furious that he was about to have them thrown into a fiery furnace. They said, "King, we're not worried. We know that our God will deliver us. But even if He doesn't, we're still not going to bow down."

This is the key: you stay in faith, believe in your dreams, believe the situation will turn around, and then declare, "Even if it doesn't happen my way, I'm still going to be happy. God, if You turn it around, or if You don't turn it around, I'm still going to give You praise." You live like that and all the forces of darkness cannot keep you from your destiny.

Conditional Trust

*Trust in him at all times, you people; pour out
your hearts to him, for God is our refuge.*

Psalm 62:8

It's easy to trust God when things are going our way. But when our prayers aren't being answered, the problem isn't turning around, and we're not seeing favor, too often we think that when it changes, we'll be happy. Conditional trust says, "God, if You answer my prayers in the way I want and according to my timetable, I'll be my best."

The problem with conditional trust is that there will always be something that's not happening fast enough, something that doesn't work out the way we want. The question is, are you mature enough to accept God's answers even when they're not what you were hoping for? God is sovereign. We're not going to understand everything that happens. Faith is trusting God when life doesn't make sense.

"Why" Questions

Why, my soul, are you downcast? Why so disturbed within me? Put your hope in God, for I will yet praise him, my Savior and my God.

Psalm 43:5

When my father's health started to go downhill, our family prayed just as hard for him as we had for my mother when she had cancer. We quoted the same Scriptures. We asked God to restore his health as He had my mother, but my father went to be with the Lord. It didn't happen the way I wanted. If I'd had conditional trust, I would have gotten upset and bitter and said, "God, why didn't You answer my prayers?"

The truth is, there will always be unanswered "why" questions. Some things are not going to make sense. You may not see it at the time, but God knows what He's doing. He has your best interest at heart. It's not random. It's a part of His plan. Dare to trust Him.

Twists and Turns

26

*A man's mind plans his way
[as he journeys through life],
but the LORD directs his steps
and establishes them.*

Proverbs 16:9 AMP

When I lost my dad, I didn't know what I would do. But I found out that God had something else for me to do that I couldn't see at the time. I didn't think I could get up in front of people. I didn't know this ability was in me. But God can see things in you that you can't see in yourself. His plan for your life is bigger than your plan. But it may not happen the way you think. God doesn't take us in a straight line. There will be twists, turns, disappointments, losses, and bad breaks. They're all a part of His plan. God is still directing your steps. Trust Him when you don't understand. Trust Him even when it feels as though you're going in the wrong direction.

Darkness into Light

You, LORD, are my lamp;
the LORD turns my
darkness into light.

2 Samuel 22:29

What I thought would be my darkest hour, the loss of my father—and I say this respectfully—in one sense turned out to be my brightest hour. It launched me into what I'm doing today, onto a new level of my destiny. But sometimes we so want things our way that we're not going to be happy unless they happen our way. That's out of balance. Anything you have to have in order to be happy the enemy can use against you.

It's good to be honest with God and tell Him your dreams. "God, this is what I want. Open these new doors." It's fine to ask, but then be mature enough to say, "But God, if it never happens, I'm still going to trust You."

March 28

In His Hands

But I am trusting you, O Lord. I said, "You alone are my God; my times are in your hands."

Psalm 31:15 TLB

We can get so consumed with what we want in life that it can become like an idol to us. "I can't be happy unless I get the house I want." It's all we think about, all we pray about, always at the forefront of our minds. Turn it over to God. Pray, believe, and then leave it in God's hands. Don't get so focused on what you want that you miss the beauty of this day. Everything may not be perfect. There may be things that need to change. But God has given you the grace to be happy today. It's very freeing when you can say, "God, it's in Your hands. I trust You unconditionally whether it works out my way or not. I trust You unconditionally even when I don't understand it."

March 29

Unconditional Trust

He will not fear bad news; his heart is steadfast, trusting [confidently relying on and believing] in the LORD.

Psalm 112:7 AMP

Previously I told the story of the three Hebrew teenagers who refused to bow down to the king's golden idol and declared to the king of Babylon, "King, we're not going to bow down. We know that our God will deliver us. But even if He doesn't, we're still not going to bow down." That's unconditional trust. It's saying, "I believe God's going to turn this situation around, but even if He doesn't, I'm still going to be happy. I believe I'm going to get the promotion. I believe my health is improving. I believe the right person is coming. But if it doesn't happen, I'm not going to get bitter or sour. I know that God is still on the throne. If He's not changing it, He has a reason. My life is in His hands."

You're Not on Your Own

The LORD will work out his plans for my life.
Psalm 138:8 NLT

Dare to trust God not just when things are going your way, but even when you don't understand it. You don't have to work out God's plan for your life. You don't have to make it happen in your own strength, try to manipulate people, or fight all your battles alone. Why don't you relax and let God work out His plan for your life? He can do it better than you can. He knows the best path. You're not going to get upset and start panicking. You know you're not doing life on our own. All the forces of darkness cannot stop what the Most High God, the Creator of the universe, has ordained. Sickness can't stop Him. Trouble at work can't stop Him. Disappointments and setbacks can't stop Him.

Giants in the Way

David said to [Goliath], "You come against me with sword and spear and javelin, but I come against you in the name of the LORD Almighty."

1 Samuel 17:45

Y ou may have a lot coming against you. Remember that the enemy is not in control of your life; God is in control. He is working out His plan. Sometimes His plan includes giants, fiery furnaces, Red Seas, Pharaohs, and other people who don't like you. Sometimes obstacles will seem insurmountable. You don't see a way, but since you know the Lord is directing your steps, you don't try to figure it all out. It may look like the end, but you have unconditional trust. "I know God will deliver me, but even if He doesn't, I'm still going to have a song of praise. I'm still going to have an attitude of faith. I'm still going to live my life happy."

Fiery Furnaces

"I see four men loose, walking in the midst of the fire; and they are not hurt, and the form of the fourth is like the Son of God."

Daniel 3:25 NKJV

You feel as though you're about to be thrown into a fire like the three Hebrew teenagers were. Sometimes His plan includes fiery furnaces. The good news is, you're not going to go in there alone. You can't be put in that fire unless God allows it.

The king had these teenagers thrown into the fiery furnace. The fire was so hot that when the guards opened the door, they were instantly killed. In a few minutes, the king came to check on them. He looked into the furnace and couldn't believe his eyes. He said, "Didn't we throw in three bound men? I see four men loosed, and one looks like the Son of God." What was that? God working out His plan for their lives!

Get God's Attention

"The eyes of the Lord search the whole earth in order to strengthen those whose hearts are fully committed to him."

2 Chronicles 16:9 NLT

The three Hebrew teenagers whom we've been considering the past few days were miraculously saved, but I wonder what the outcome would have been if they had had conditional trust. "God, if You deliver us from this fire, if You do it our way, we'll stay in faith." Maybe the furnace would have been the end. Maybe we wouldn't be talking about them today.

If you want to get God's attention, if you want Him to take you where you've never dreamed and turn impossible situations around, be like those teenagers and have a statement of faith: "I know God will deliver me from this fire." But then follow it up with, "But even if He doesn't, I'm still going to honor Him. I'm still going to be my best."

Through the Trial

"You'll not be harvested until it's time."

Job 5:26 TLB

Like the biblical hero Job, you may be facing a serious illness, but if it's not your time to go, you're not going to go. God has the final say. Right now He is working out His plan for your life. There may be some dark places. Are you going to trust Him only if He takes away all the thorns and does it your way?

When you have unconditional trust in God to take you through the trial, you take away all the enemy's power and you can't be defeated. You may have challenges that look bigger and stronger than you can overcome. On your own, you don't have a chance. Don't be intimidated. The forces for you are greater than the forces against you.

His Ways

*"As the heavens are higher than the earth,
so are my ways higher than your ways and
my thoughts than your thoughts."*

Isaiah 55:9

When I look back over my life, I see that many things haven't turned out the way I'd thought they would. I had a plan. I had it all figured out. I told God what to do, when to do it, what I needed, whom to use, and how to get me there. I gave Him good information, my very best. The funny thing is, God didn't take my advice. He had His own plan. I found that God's plan is always better than my plan. His ways have always been more rewarding, more fulfilling, and bigger than my ways. If God had done everything I asked, answered my prayers the way I wanted and according to my timetable, it would have limited my destiny. I wouldn't be where I am.

Closed Doors

5

*"The words of the holy one,…
who has the key of David, who
opens and no one will shut,
who shuts and no one opens."*

Revelation 3:7 ESV

Don't be discouraged over something that
didn't work out the way you wanted.
God knows what He's doing. You may not
see it now, but one day when you see what
God was up to, you'll be glad He closed the
doors. You'll thank Him for not answering
your prayers. The longer I live, the more I
pray, "God, let not my will but Your will be
done." I don't get frustrated when a door
closes or things aren't changing as fast as I
would like. I know that God is in control. As
long as you're honoring Him and being your
best, at the right time God will get you to
where you're supposed to be. It may not be
where you thought, but God is going to take
you further than you ever imagined.

Hold Tightly, Hold Loosely

*Does the clay say to the potter,
"What are you making?"*

Isaiah 45:9

Many years ago Victoria and I were certain we'd found our dream house. We prayed over it, thanking God that it was ours, and made an offer. But the seller rejected our offer and sold it to somebody else. We were deeply disappointed, but if we're only going to be happy if God does it our way, that's not trusting Him; that's giving God orders.

I believe in praying bold prayers for our dreams, believing for big things. But I've learned to let God do it His way. Hold tightly to what God put in your heart, but hold loosely to how it's going to happen. Don't get set in your ways. Don't be discouraged because it hasn't happened the way you thought. God is working out His plan for your life.

April 7

More Than You Imagine

Don't fret or worry. Instead of worrying, pray.
Let petitions and praises shape your worries into
prayers, letting God know your concerns.

Philippians 4:6 MSG

Have you ever felt as though God had let you down? He could have opened the door that closed. You're frustrated. Why don't you put your life in His hands? He knows what's best for you. He can see things that we can't see.

A few months after we lost the "dream house" I mentioned in yesterday's reading, we purchased another house. A few years after that, we sold half of that property for more than we paid for the whole property. We ended up building a new house there. God blessed us in ways greater than we'd ever imagined. Now sometimes I'll drive back by that other house I wanted so badly and say, "Lord, thank You for closing that door. Thank You that it didn't work out."

April 8

Embrace Where You Are

This is the day the LORD has made;
we will rejoice and be glad in it.

Psalm 118:24 NKJV

You could save yourself a lot of frustration if you'd learn to have unconditional trust. The closed doors, the disappointments, the delays—it's all working for you. And yes, it's good to be determined. Be persistent. But let God do it His way. If He's not changing it, not removing it, not opening it, don't fight it. Learn to embrace where you are. He's given you the grace not just to be there but to be there with a good attitude. If you're going to pass the test, keep a smile on your face. Keep a song in your heart. Keep passion in your spirit. Don't drag through the day the Lord has made. He's working out His plan for your life. He's going to get you to where you're supposed to be.

The Trust Test

*And He said, "Do not lay
your hand on the lad, or do
anything to him; for now I
know that you fear God…"*

Genesis 22:12 NKJV

Abraham was seventy-five years old
when God promised him "to become a
great nation" (see Gen. 12), and he waited
twenty-five years before the birth of his son
Isaac. He and his wife, Sarah, had prayed,
believed, stood in faith, and finally seen
the promise come to pass. You can imagine
how Abraham must have felt many years
later when God told him to take Isaac to
the top of a mountain and sacrifice him.
Isaac was the fulfillment of the promise
God had given him. Now God was asking
him to put his dream on the altar. Abraham
didn't understand it, but he was obedient.
He passed the trust test. And just as he was
about to follow through, God stopped him
and said, "Now I can see you trust Me more
than anything."

As an Offering

*Take your everyday,
ordinary life—your sleeping,
eating, going-to-work,
and walking-around life—
and place it before God
as an offering.*

Romans 12:1 MSG

As we saw with Abraham in yesterday's
reading, there will be times when God
asks us to put our dream on the altar. We
have to show Him that we don't have to have
the house to be happy. If we don't have the
baby, we're not going to live bitter and sour.
You're believing for your health to improve,
but when you can say, "If it doesn't get
better, God, I'm still going to honor You.
I'm still going to be my best," you are doing
what Abraham did. You are putting your
dream on the altar. God wants to see if you'll
trust Him when you don't understand. And
when He sees that you don't have to have it,
many times God will give you back what you
were willing to give up.

With Your Whole Heart

Trust GOD from the bottom of your heart; don't try to figure out everything on your own....he's the one who will keep you on track.

Proverbs 3:5–6 MSG

Living worried, frustrated, and disappointed takes our passion, steals our joy, and can keep us from seeing God's favor. Sometimes the closed doors and the disappointments are simply a test. God wants to see if we'll trust Him when life doesn't make sense.

Will you do the right thing when it's hard? Will you trust God when the situation isn't what you'd thought? Will you trust Him when you don't understand it? God said to Abraham, "Because you did not withhold your only son, I will surely bless you and make your descendants as numerous as the sand on the seashore." When you do as Abraham did and pass the trust test, God will not only give you the desires of your heart, He'll do more than you ask or think.

According to His Will

*This is the confidence we
have in approaching God:
that if we ask anything
according to his will,
he hears us.*

1 John 5:14

APRIL 12

Are you living frustrated because your
prayers aren't being answered the way you
want? Your plans aren't working out? Take
the pressure off. God is in control. He's still
on the throne. You're not always going to
understand it. If you did, it wouldn't take any
faith. I can tell you firsthand that with some
of the things that are not working out in your
life now, one day you'll be saying, "Lord,
thank You that it didn't work out my way."

I'm asking you to trust Him unconditionally. If you'll do this, I believe God is
going to work out His plan for your life.
He's going to open the right doors, bring the
right people to you, turn negative situations
around, and take you to the fullness of
your destiny.

The Big Picture

*"I make known the end from the beginning,
from ancient times, what is still to come.
I say, 'My purpose will stand...'"*

Isaiah 46:10

We all go through difficulties, setbacks, and loss. Pain is a part of life, and it often feels like a dark place. It's easy to get discouraged and think, *God, why did this happen?* But I've learned to not put a question mark where God has put a period. All of us live through things we don't understand. One reason is that we can't see the big picture for our lives. It's like isolating one piece of a jigsaw puzzle and thinking, *This piece is a mistake. It's nothing like the picture on the front of the box.* But the fact is, it has a perfect place. When all the pieces come together, it's going to fit right in. You just can't see it now because the other pieces are not in place.

We See Imperfectly

Now we see things imperfectly, like puzzling reflections in a mirror, but then we will see everything with perfect clarity.

1 Corinthians 13:12 NLT

Sometimes we look at the painful times in our lives—the times when we're hurting, we're lonely, we're undergoing medical treatment, and when on the surface the pieces of our life don't make sense—and think they can't be a part of God's plan. You have to trust that even then, God doesn't make any mistakes. He's already designed your life and laid out every piece, down to the smallest detail. He never said we would understand everything along the way. God didn't promise that there wouldn't be any pain, suffering, or disappointment. But He did promise that it would all work out for our good. That piece that's painful, that doesn't look as though it makes sense—when everything comes together, it's going to fit perfectly in place.

APRIL

15

Changed for Good

"Here on earth you will have many trials and sorrows. But take heart, because I have overcome the world."

John 16:33 NLT

Pain will change us. Difficulties, heartache, suffering—they don't leave us the same. When I went through the loss of my father, I didn't come out of that experience the same person. I was changed. If you go through a divorce or a legal battle, or have a friend who betrays you, eventually the experience will pass and you will get through it, but you will be different. The key is what you do in your times of pain. You can come out bitter, or you can come out better. You can come out with a chip on your shoulder, or you can come out with a greater trust in God. You can come out defeated, having given up on your dreams, or you can come out blessed, looking for the new opportunities in front of you.

Refined

APRIL

16

"Have you not put a hedge around him and his household and everything he has?"

Job 1:10

God is not only in control of our lives, He's in control of the enemy. Satan had to ask for permission from God before he could test Job. The enemy may turn on the furnace, but God controls how much heat, how much pain, how much adversity we will face. He knows what we can handle. If it is going to harm us rather than help us, He dials it back. You could easily let the tough times overwhelm you. It's helpful to remind yourself, "I may be in the furnace, but I know who's controlling the temperature. The God who is for me and not against me is not going to let it defeat me. I can handle it." You have that attitude, and you're going to come out refined, purified, prepared, and stronger.

April 17

Greater Trust

We also glory in our sufferings, because we know that suffering produces perseverance; perseverance, character; and character, hope.

Romans 5:3–4

You've heard the saying "No pain, no gain." If everything were always easy, we wouldn't be prepared for our destiny. Some of the situations and pressures that I face today would have overwhelmed me if I'd faced them ten years ago. I couldn't have handled it back then. God knows exactly what you need and when you need it. Every struggle is making you stronger. Every difficulty is growing you up. You may not like it, but every painful time is developing something in you that can be developed only in the tough times. My challenge is, don't just go through it; grow through it. That difficulty is an opportunity to develop character, to gain a greater trust in God. Don't complain about the pain, because without the pain you wouldn't reach the fullness of your destiny.

April 18

· · · · · · · · · · · · · ·

Created for Adversity

*Since Christ suffered and underwent pain,
you must have the same attitude he did;
you must be ready to suffer, too.*

1 Peter 4:1 TLB

In 1982, researchers aboard the space shuttle *Columbia* did an experiment with honeybees. They took them up into space to study the effects of weightlessness on them. According to a NASA memo, the bees "were unable to fly normally and tumbled into weightlessness." Then it was reported that "the bees have all gotten stationary." One can imagine that they just floated through the air with great ease, having a great time while not having to use their wings. Perhaps they thought, *This is the life. This is the way we were created to live—no struggle, no hardship, no pain.* But they all died. You might say that they enjoyed the ride, but they died. They may have loved having it easy, having no adversity, but they weren't created for that, and neither were we.

Stronger Than Ever

19

After you have suffered a little while, our God…will come and pick you up, and set you firmly in place, and make you stronger than ever.

1 Peter 5:10 TLB

We weren't made to float through life on flowery beds of ease. We'd love to not have any pain, suffering, bad breaks, betrayals, or loss, but that's not reality. Difficulties will come, and pain is a part of life, so keep the right perspective. In the tough dark times, God is getting you prepared. If it were too much, God would dial back the intensity. He has His hand on the thermostat. Quit telling yourself that you can't take it. You're not weak. You are well able. You are full of can-do power. You are armed with strength for this battle. The reason the fire is so hot is that there's something big in your future. God is growing you up. He's getting you ready to receive blessings, favor, and increase as you've never seen.

Count It All Joy

Count it all joy when you fall into various trials, knowing that the testing of your faith produces patience.

James 1:2–3 NKJV

There is purpose in your pain. God allows the pain, but He doesn't say, "Let Me give them some pain to make their life miserable." He uses it for a purpose. We're not always going to understand it. "Why did I get sick? Why did my loved one not make it? Why did my marriage not work?" I can't answer the whys, but I can tell you that if God allowed it, He knows how to bring good out of it. This is what faith is all about. "God, I don't like this pain and darkness, but I trust You. I believe You're in control. I'm going to grow through it and keep a good attitude. I'm going to count it all joy, knowing that this pain is going to lead to my gain."

Learn from It

A wise man will hear and increase learning…

Proverbs 1:5 NKJV

Sometimes we bring pain on ourselves. We make poor choices, get into a relationship that we knew would not be good, or get in over our head in our spending, and then there's the pain—we're dealing with the consequences. God is full of mercy, and He'll always give us the grace to get through it. But in order not to waste the pain and go through it again, you have to learn the lesson.

A man I know struggled with diabetes for years and ended up in the hospital for a month. When I saw him afterward, he said, "That time in the hospital was a wake-up call. I've lost forty pounds, changed my diet, exercise every day, and feel like a new man." He's not wasting the pain. He learned the lesson.

122

Before You Let Go

I applied my heart to what I observed and learned a lesson from what I saw.

Proverbs 24:32

APRIL 22

We talk about how important it is to let go of the past, to let go of the divorce, the failure, the bad break, and that's true. But before you let go of the negative event, you need to remember the lesson that you learned from the experience. You're doing yourself a disservice if you go through a painful time and don't come out with what you were supposed to gain. I talked to a man who was about to get married for the fourth time. I'm not judging him, but he made one statement that was very telling. He said, "All my wives have run around on me." I didn't say it, but I thought that maybe the lesson he needs to learn is to be careful about the kind of women to whom he gravitates.

Don't Repeat Mistakes

...fools repeat their folly.
Proverbs 26:11

There's a lesson in life's pain. Don't keep repeating the same mistakes. Consider a guy who was driving his car, had an accident, and got out upset. He went over to the other driver and said, "Lady, why don't you watch where you're going? You're the fifth person who's run into me today!" He's going to keep experiencing that pain until he gets big enough to look inside and say, "You know what, I have to learn how to drive."

Are you bringing pain on yourself? Are you struggling with relationships that don't last, perhaps because you keep saying everything you feel like saying? The pain will stop if you learn the lesson and zip it up. Be big enough to say, "Here's where I missed it, but I'm not going to do it again."

Where God Puts a Period

"I will fulfill the number of your days."

Exodus 23:26 NKJV

Sometimes we experience pain that has nothing to do with our choices. It isn't our fault. We are doing the right thing, and the wrong thing happens.

My mother was raising five children and pastoring the church with my father when she was diagnosed with terminal cancer. Not only was that physically uncomfortable, it was emotionally painful to think about leaving her children and husband. But my mother had learned that where God puts a period, she shouldn't put a question mark. She said, "God, You said the number of my days You will fulfill. My life is in Your hands." It didn't happen overnight, but my mother got better and better. Today not only is she healthy but God birthed something new in her—a prayer ministry for the sick!

Share It with Others

*The God of all comfort,
who comforts us in all our
tribulation, that we may be
able to comfort those who
are in any trouble...*

2 Corinthians 1:3–4 NKJV

There are times when God will allow us to go through a painful season so He can birth something new on the inside. If you go through something you don't understand, God allowed this to happen because He trusts you. He knows He can count on you to take the same comfort, the same healing, the same encouragement that helped you overcome this trouble, and share it with others.

My mother was not only healed of cancer, but, out of that painful time, God birthed something new in her. She started going around praying for other people who were sick. She goes up to the medical center every week and has healing services in the chapel. The very thing that tried to destroy her was what God used to push her to a new level of her destiny.

Purpose in Your Pain

"What? Shall we receive only pleasant things from the hand of God and never anything unpleasant?"

Job 2:10 TLB

Maybe you've gone through something you don't understand—sickness, abuse, infertility, raising a difficult child. It's painful. Life didn't turn out the way you'd hoped. It's easy to have a victim mentality and think, *If God is good, why did this happen to me?* It's because God knows He can trust you with it. The forces of darkness wanted to take you out, but God said, "Not so fast. That's My son, that's My daughter. I have an assignment for them." And God is saying this about you: "It's difficult, but I know what you're made of. It's painful, but in the end I'm not only going to bring you out stronger, increased, and promoted. I'm going to use you to help others who are struggling in that same area." There is purpose in your pain.

April 27

Rise Up

See, darkness covers the earth and thick darkness is over the peoples, but the LORD rises upon you and his glory appears over you.

Isaiah 60:2

In May 1980, Candy Lightner's daughter Cari was struck and killed by a drunk driver who was a repeat offender. This mother was devastated and didn't think she could go on. But fueled by a mother's rage, she started an organization called Mothers Against Drunk Driving. Thirty-eight years later, it is one of the country's largest activist organizations and has saved hundreds of thousands of lives, changed laws, and influenced public awareness and policy.

Candy Lightner didn't waste her pain. She could have sat around in the dark place of self-pity and given up on her dreams, but she didn't put a question mark where God had put a period. Today she's affecting the world. The enemy meant her experience for harm, but God used it for good.

April 28

Help Others

*If you do these things, God will shed his own
glorious light upon you. He will heal you;
your godliness will lead you forward.*

Isaiah 58:8 TLB

Most of us are not going to experience
something as tragic as Candy Lightner
(yesterday's reading), but if she could take
one of life's greatest pains and turn it around
to become a force for good, then you and I
can find the purpose in our pain. Don't get
caught up wondering, "Where does this piece
of my puzzle go? It's ugly, and it doesn't make
sense." Keep moving forward. Go out as she
did and find somebody you can help. Healing
comes when you get outside yourself and help
others. As long as you stay focused on your
pain, what you lost, what didn't work out,
you're going to get stuck. There's a blessing
in that pain. You are uniquely qualified.
You have something to give others. You can
comfort those who are going through what
you've been through.

Let Your Light Shine

"…let your light shine before others…"
Matthew 5:16

I know a lady who believed there was a purpose to her painful cancer diagnosis, took the chemo for one difficult year, and is cancer-free. Now she goes back to the hospital as a volunteer and tells other people fighting cancer, "I know what you're going through. God brought me through the chemo, and He can do it for you." She's not wasting her pain. Her test has become her testimony.

We've all been through difficult things, but God made a way where we didn't see a way. If it weren't for His goodness, we wouldn't be here. God is counting on us to let our light shine through the dark places. What you've been through will help somebody else get through it. Be on the lookout for others you can encourage.

Encourage and Comfort

Therefore encourage and comfort one another and build up one another.

1 Thessalonians 5:11 AMP

Lolo Jones, a two-time World Indoor Champion in the sixty-meter hurdles, went to the 2008 Olympics heavily favored to win the gold medal in the hundred-meter hurdles. But she hit the ninth hurdle and slightly fell, which allowed another runner to pass her. She had worked her whole life for that twelve-second race and lost. In an interview she said, in effect, "It's very painful, but I know now I can help other people who have fallen." She's not wasting her pain.

When you've been through something, you're uniquely qualified to help somebody else in that situation. Some experiences help us grow, mature, and come up higher. Then there are times when God will allow us to go through a difficult time so later on we can be instrumental in helping others overcome.

Offer Comfort

"Comfort, yes, comfort my people," says your God.

Isaiah 40:1 TLB

Can God trust you with pain? Or will you get discouraged and say, "I don't understand why this is happening to me"? I say this respectfully: it's not all about you. What if God has allowed this difficulty so three years down the road you can help somebody else move forward? Can He trust you? When I lost my father, that was painful. But you can't imagine how many people tell me, "Joel, when you talk about how much you loved your father, and how you stepped up and kept moving forward, that helped me to move forward when my loved one died." The comfort I received during that loss I now can pass on to others. We've all been through loss, pain, and struggle. You may not like it, but there's a purpose to the pain.

Don't Focus on the Pain

Because of the joy awaiting [Jesus], he endured the cross.

Hebrews 12:2 NLT

I saw a news story about a healthy woman who started feeling nauseated, couldn't sleep well at night, then her back started hurting and her feet were swelling. The doctor thought it was a virus that would pass. Months later she had so much pain that her husband rushed her to the emergency room, where she delivered her first baby boy.

Like her, there are many times when we're pregnant but we don't know it. All we feel is the pain. The pain is a sign that you're about to give birth. If you'll stay in faith, you'll give birth to new strength, new talents, new ministry, new relationships. When you're in a difficult season, don't focus on the pain. Focus on the fact that a new level is coming.

Waste No Pain

*As you know, it was because of an illness that
I first preached the gospel to you…*

Galatians 4:13

My friend Craig was the head of our children's ministry. After he and his wife, Samantha, had their third child, they realized something wasn't right. Little Connor was diagnosed with autism. Of course they loved Connor unconditionally, but it wasn't what they had been expecting. They were discouraged, but they didn't waste their pain. Craig talked to me about how parents couldn't come and attend a service if their special needs children required constant attention. He said, "Why don't we start a special needs class?" We started the Champions Club, and within the first few months, three hundred new families joined the church! Then other churches heard about it, and Craig helped them launch their own special needs ministries. Today there are over thirty Champions Clubs in seven different nations.

From Pain to Gain

You know we call those blessed [happy, spiritually prosperous, favored by God] who were steadfast and endured [difficult circumstances].

James 5:11 AMP

When you experience pain, don't get discouraged. Get ready, because you're about to give birth. There's a gift in that pain. There's a ministry in that pain. There's a blessing in that pain. Don't waste it. Look for opportunities. God is counting on you to help others facing the same thing. Can God trust you with pain? Will you say, "God, I may not understand this, but I trust You."

Remember, God has His hand on the thermostat. He has a purpose for it. Don't just go through it, grow through it. If you'll do this, your pain is going to be turned into your gain. You're going to come out stronger, promoted, and increased. Out of that pain you're going to give birth to a new level of your destiny.

MAY

5

Blessed by Enemies

So David triumphed over the Philistine with a sling and a stone; without a sword in his hand he struck down the Philistine.

1 Samuel 17:50

If it weren't for Goliath, David would be known only as a shepherd boy. Goliath was strategically placed in David's path—not to defeat him, but to promote him. Without Goliath, David would never have taken the throne. What may look like a setback is really a setup to get you to your throne.

We all know that God can bless us. But what we don't always realize is that God can use our enemies to bless us. What you think is a disappointment someone has caused— that person who left you, that coworker who's trying to make you look bad, that friend who betrayed you—you may not like it, but you couldn't reach your destiny without it. It's all a part of God's plan to get you to where you're supposed to be.

It's Not about Pleasing People

Be assured that when we speak to you we're not after crowd approval— only God approval.

1 Thessalonians 2:4 MSG

After David defeated Goliath, you never read anything more about Goliath. He was created for David's purpose. God could have used King Saul, who had the authority, to promote David. All God had to do was move on Saul's heart and tell him, "Promote that young man." But God chose to bless David through his enemy Goliath, not through his friends. That's why we don't have to play up to people and try to convince them to like us, thinking, *Maybe they'll give me a good break.* God doesn't have to use your friends or associates. He can use your enemies, your critics, the people who are trying to push you down. So don't complain about your enemies, because God will use them to push you up.

May 7

Step Up

*You [my enemy] pushed me violently so that
I was falling, but the LORD helped me.*

Psalm 118:13 AMP

Part of Goliath's destiny was to establish who David was. In the same way, God has lined up divine connections, people who will be good to you, encourage you, and push you forward. He's also lined up people who will try to stop you, people who will try to make you look bad and discourage you. There are Goliaths ordained to come across your path. If you don't understand this principle, you'll get discouraged and think, *God, why is this happening to me?* That opposition is not there to stop you; it's there to establish you. When you overcome, not only will you step up to a new level of your destiny, but everyone around you will see the favor of God on your life.

May 8

All Things

*I can do all things through Christ
who strengthens me.*

Philippians 4:13 NKJV

When we received word that the city
leaders of Houston were thinking
about selling the Compaq Center, I knew
it was supposed to be ours. But there was
opposition to our getting the building, and
in particular one high-powered business
executive who said, "It will be a cold day in
hell before Lakewood gets that building."
That executive was one of those Goliaths
whom God strategically placed in our path.

When I heard how much he was against
us, a new fire, a holy determination, rose up
inside me. Every time things got tough and
I was tempted to think it wasn't going to
work out, I would recall his words, *a cold day
in hell*, and instantly get my passion back.
Sometimes God will put an enemy in your
life to keep you stirred up.

A Table Prepared

*You prepare a table before
me in the presence of
my enemies.*

Psalm 23:5

When God brings you through the dark
valley of opposition, He's going to do
it in such a way that all your enemies can
see He has blessed you. Lakewood is on the
second-busiest freeway in the nation. Every
time that businessman who said we'd never
get the Compaq Center drives by, I can
imagine something whispers in his ear, "It's
a cold day in hell."

You may be up against a similar enemy
right now—an enemy to your health, your
finances, a relationship. Have this new
perspective: God is preparing the table
right now, where even your enemies—the
doubters, the critics, the people who said
it wouldn't work out—are going to see you
blessed, healed, promoted, vindicated, in a
position of honor and influence.

Without the Betrayal

Jesus said to Judas, "Friend, do what you came for."

Matthew 26:50 AMP

When Judas betrayed and tried to stop Jesus, it seemed like a bad break. But had he not betrayed Jesus, there wouldn't have been a crucifixion, and without the cross there wouldn't have been a resurrection, and without a resurrection we wouldn't have redemption. The man who sold Jesus out for thirty pieces of silver was critical to His destiny.

What am I saying? Don't complain about that person who betrayed you. If they walked away, they didn't set you back; they set you up. If that had not happened, you wouldn't get to where you're supposed to be. If they tried to push you down and lied about you, it may not have been fair, but nothing happens by accident. If God allowed it, He knows how to use it for your good.

It's Not an Accident

Jesus knew that the Father had given him authority over everything and that he had come from God and would return to God.

John 13:3 NLT

When Jesus was betrayed by Judas, what if He had gotten upset and said, "God, I'm Your Son. How could You allow one of My main disciples to betray Me?" Jesus knew Judas was going to betray Him, but He didn't try to stop him. He said at their last supper together, "The one to whom I give this bread is going to betray Me." He handed it to Judas and said, "Go, do what you're going to do quickly." Jesus understood that betrayal was a part of His destiny. Too often we fight what doesn't go our way; we get upset and become bitter. But the longer I live, the more I realize that nothing happens by accident. If you keep the right attitude, God will even use the opposition to bless you.

Prove Them Wrong

And the Lord's servant must not be quarrelsome but must be kind to everyone, able to teach, not resentful.

2 Timothy 2:24

MAY 12

I talked to a well-known minister one time. For over fifty years he had gone around the world doing so much good. But in his hometown, even though he could do a hundred things right, the local newspaper editors constantly found something they didn't like and made a big deal about it. He had an interesting perspective. He told me, "If it weren't for that newspaper, I wouldn't have accomplished as much. It not only kept me on my knees, but it gave me the fuel to prove them wrong." Toward the end of his life, that paper's editors finally had a change of heart. They wrote a big front-page article that celebrated everything he had done. It was as though God had waited on purpose because He knew that enemy was making him better, more determined and more diligent.

Iron Sharpens Iron

*As iron sharpens iron, so one person
sharpens another.*

Proverbs 27:17

There are some things we don't like, some things we may even be praying for God to take away from us, but if He removed them, we wouldn't reach our highest potential. That opposition is making you stronger. Those people who try to push you down, the betrayal, the disappointment— none of these can keep you from your destiny. God has the final say. If He hasn't removed it, that means it's working for you.

God strategically places the Goliaths, the Judases, the critics, the opposition in our lives. Without Goliath, you won't take your throne; without Judas, you won't reach your destiny; without the naysayers, you won't become all you were created to be.

Be True to Your Words

*"But that you may know that the Son of Man
has power on earth to forgive sins…
I say to you, arise…"*

Mark 2:10–11 NKJV

In the Scripture, four men carried a paralyzed man to see Jesus. When they arrived at the house, it was so crowded inside they had to take him up on the roof and let him down through the ceiling. At one point Jesus said to the man, "Your sins have been forgiven." Some of the religious leaders were offended and began to murmur, "Who does He think He is? Only God can forgive sins." Challenged by His critics, Jesus said to them, "Which is easier to say, 'Your sins are forgiven,' or 'Arise, take up your bed and walk'?" To prove to them that He was the Son of God, He turned to the paralyzed man and told him to rise up. The man stood up, perfectly well, and I'm sure the religious leaders nearly passed out.

God Sees and Hears

Jesus knew immediately what they were thinking, so he asked them, "Why do you question this in your hearts?"

Mark 2:8 NLT

In yesterday's reading, if the religious leaders had not been murmuring and criticizing Jesus, maybe this man wouldn't have been healed. Jesus could have just forgiven his sins and moved on. But right in the midst of their murmuring, Jesus healed him. When people are talking about you, trying to push you down and keep you in a dark place, don't worry—God sees and hears them. They're putting you in position to be blessed in a greater way. You don't have to straighten them out. Don't get involved in battles that don't matter. Let them talk. Just as with this man, God will use your enemies to bless you. Some of the favor you've seen, some of the good breaks, happened because of the people who tried to stop you. They put you in position for promotion.

Increase Is on the Way

*Consider him who endured
such opposition from sinners,
so that you will not grow
weary and lose heart.*

Hebrews 12:3

A man told me his business had dwindled down to nothing, then one of his main competitors had gone on a radio show and talked about it in a very unfavorable light. It looked as though that would be the final blow that put this business under, but that drew attention to his business, and new clients started calling. Today his business has surpassed the competitor's company.

I've learned to thank God for my enemies. Without Goliath, David might not have taken the throne; without that executive who was against us, we might not have our building. You need to see every enemy, every adversity, every disappointment in a new light: the opposition is not there to defeat you, it's there to increase you, to make you better.

May 17

Prosper through Adversity

*Isaac planted crops in that land and
[during a famine year] reaped a hundredfold,
because the LORD blessed him.*

Genesis 26:12

In the early nineteen hundreds, a tiny insect called the boll weevil was destroying the cotton crops in Alabama and nothing was working to get rid of them. Eventually all that the farmers could do was watch their livelihood be eaten away—a very dark place to be in. But one day a farmer had an idea to plant peanuts and convinced others to try it as well. They discovered that the boll weevils didn't like the taste of peanuts. Their crops took off in a way they had never seen. They made more money off peanuts in a few months than they would normally make all year long. In fact, when the boll weevils were later diminished, many of the farmers stuck with the peanuts. God used the boll weevil to bless them with prosperity.

May 18

Stepping-stones

"Sit at my right hand until I make your enemies a footstool for your feet."

Psalm 110:1

Like the farmers in yesterday's reading, you may be dealing with some boll weevils in your life right now. My encouragement is that you stay in faith—peanuts are coming. What you think is a setback is really God setting you up to do something new. Don't sit around complaining about what didn't work out and who did you wrong—that's just a boll weevil. What looks as though it's there to destroy or hurt you will launch you to a new level. God said that He would make your enemies your footstools. That means that when something comes against you— persecution, betrayal, disappointment— instead of letting it be a stumbling block that makes you go down, if you'll stay in faith, God will turn stumbling blocks into stepping-stones that cause you to go up.

Don't Be Intimidated

Don't be intimidated in any way by your enemies.

Philippians 1:28 NLT

I was the smallest player on our Little League baseball team. When an opposing coach saw how small I was, he shifted his outfielders in right behind the infield. When I saw that, I thought, *He doesn't know that I am a child of the Most High God. I can do all things through Christ.* When the pitcher threw the ball, I swung as though I were ten feet tall and drove the ball over their heads to the fence. I made an inside-the-park home run! And the next time I got up to bat, that coach told his outfielders to back up!

Don't be intimidated by what somebody says or by how big the obstacle is. You are full of can-do power. The greatest force in the universe is on your side.

Multiplication

*The more they afflicted
them, the more they
multiplied and grew.*

Exodus 1:12 NKJV

After the death of Joseph, the people of
Israel living in Egypt were blessed and
increased greatly in numbers, to the point
that many years later, Pharaoh feared them
and put them under slave masters to oppress
them with forced labor. But the Scripture
says, "The more Pharaoh afflicted them,
the more the Israelites multiplied." Pharaoh
thought he was stopping them, but in fact
he was increasing them. Sometimes when
God wants to promote you, He doesn't send
you a good break; He sends you an enemy.
He'll cause a supervisor perhaps, to turn
up the heat. Don't get discouraged—the
more opposition, the more you're going to
increase. We may not like it, but we grow
under pressure, our character is developed,
and we discover talent that we didn't know
we had.

Pressure Will Increase You

But this [great pressure, far beyond our ability to endure] happened that we might not rely on ourselves but on God...

2 Corinthians 1:9

When you need the water to shoot farther out of your garden hose, you put your thumb over the end of the hose and restrict the flow of the water. When you restrict the water, the same amount shoots out, but because it's under so much more pressure, it goes many times farther.

In the same way, when the enemy puts you under pressure, he thinks it's going to stop you. What he doesn't realize is that all that pressure is going to cause you to shoot out further. When you feel restricted, when you face opposition, don't be discouraged. Get ready to shoot out. Get ready for new levels. Get ready for promotion. That pressure is not going to stop you; it's going to increase you.

Triumph over It

"I am the Living One; I was dead, and now look, I am alive for ever and ever! And I hold the keys of death and Hades."

Revelation 1:18

MAY 22

When Jesus was about to be crucified, He went to the Garden of Gethsemane, which literally means "the place of pressing." It was an olive grove. The only way to get the valuable oil out of the olives is to press them. If you're never put under pressure, if you never have to stretch your faith, endure, overcome, and persevere, you won't tap into the treasures God put on the inside.

On a Friday, Jesus was nailed to the cross—incredible pressure. On Saturday, He was in the grave, fighting the forces of darkness—restricted. But on Sunday morning, He came shooting up out of that grave. Death couldn't hold Him down. One message of the resurrection is that God uses our enemies to bless us.

For the Best

My troubles turned out all for the best—
they forced me to learn from your textbook.

Psalm 119:71 MSG

Maybe you feel restricted today, pressured, as though you're being squeezed. The pressure is going to cause you to shoot out. When you see where God takes you—the favor, the blessing, the promotion—you're going to look back and say it "turned out all for the best." David would tell you that it was good that Goliath showed up. The Israelites would tell you that it was good that Pharaoh restricted them.

Now stay in faith, for God has your back. He wouldn't allow the pressure if it weren't going to work for your good. You're about to shoot out, stronger, healthier, promoted, vindicated, and better off than you were before. One day you will say, "That enemy didn't defeat me; that enemy blessed me."

Blossoms

The desert and the parched land will be glad;
the wilderness will rejoice and blossom.

Isaiah 35:1

We put mulch on our flower beds at home that includes a fertilizer that uses manure as one of its main ingredients. It's waste, and for several days after we apply it, it smells really bad. But in a month or two, the smell is long gone and the plants are blooming and blossoming. That fertilizer gives the plants valuable nutrients and minerals that they could not get on their own.

In a similar way, we all go through things in life that stink. We don't like what has happened; something wasn't fair. You need to have a new perspective: that's just fertilizer. The stinky stuff—the betrayal, the disappointment, the loss—is getting you prepared for new growth, to bloom, to blossom, to become all you were created to be.

Stick with It

25

"I promise that I'll bless you with everything I have—bless and bless and bless!" Abraham stuck it out and got everything that had been promised to him.

Hebrews 6:13–15 MSG

I'd love to tell you that if you'll just trust God and be your best, you'll sail through life with no difficulties, but that's not reality. You're going to have some manure coming your way. What I want you to see is that it's not working against you; it's working for you. Instead of getting depressed and thinking, *This stinks. I can't believe this happened,* have this attitude: *It's just more fertilizer. God's getting me prepared for something greater.* The truth is, you cannot reach your highest potential without fertilizer. If you'll go through the stink with the right attitude and not let it sour your life, God will take what was meant for your harm and use it for your good. You'll come into a new season of growth and opportunities for new levels of your destiny.

Get Ready | MAY

"Get yourself ready!"

Jeremiah 1:17

26

You may feel as though you've already had more than your share of stinky stuff—bad breaks, disappointments, broken dreams. Be encouraged, because that means you have a lot of fertilizer. God is getting you ready to go where you've never been. This is not the time to feel sorry for yourself, thinking about all you've been through. This is the time to get ready. God allowed that fertilizer to get you prepared for where you could not go on your own. It deposited something on the inside that you could only get by going through it.

Quit complaining about the fertilizer—about who hurt you and what didn't work out—and all the manure that got dumped on you. Without the smelly stuff, you couldn't reach your destiny.

May 27

Beat the Odds

But thanks be to God! He gives us the victory through our Lord Jesus Christ.

1 Corinthians 15:57

There was a young lady whose father died when she was six years old, whose mother was ill and required constant care, and whose little brother needed her to be the mom. It seemed that this hardship would put her behind. But just because something is unfair doesn't mean that God doesn't still have an amazing future in front in you. This young lady didn't have a victim mentality; she had a victor mentality. It was hard, but she just kept being her best, not letting negative thoughts talk her out of her dreams. Despite all the odds stacked against her, she excelled in high school, received a full scholarship to a major university, got her master's, and then she earned a doctorate degree. Today she's extremely successful in the corporate world and happily married with three beautiful children.

Overcome

The person who wins out over the world's ways is simply the one who believes Jesus is the Son of God.

1 John 5:4 MSG

Why do some people who grow up in difficult situations struggle through life, living defeated, discouraged, and always overcome by problems, while others, such as the young lady in yesterday's reading, overcome the odds, flourish, and see God's goodness in amazing ways? It's in how we approach life. We all have stinky stuff; we all have unfair situations, things we don't like. You can get bitter, discouraged, and sour, or you can see it as fertilizer and say, "This difficulty is not going to defeat me; it's going to promote me. It's not going to hinder me; it's going to help me." God wouldn't have allowed it unless He had a purpose. Don't just go through it, grow through it. Recognize that it's making you stronger. You're developing character, perseverance, trust, and confidence.

Glory to Be Revealed

I consider that our present sufferings are not worth comparing with the glory that will be revealed in us.

Romans 8:18

A difficult, dark time in your life doesn't have to keep you from your destiny. Actually, it can do just the opposite. It can propel you into your destiny. What stinks in your life right now, and what you don't like, can be the very thing that promotes you and causes you to blossom. Without the fertilizer, you couldn't reach your highest potential. Don't complain about the stink; there's promotion in that stink. Don't get sour because of the smelly stuff; there's a new level in that smelly stuff. Don't be discouraged by the manure. You may not like it, but that's fertilizer.

The manure doesn't smell good, but it has nutrients and minerals; it's making you stronger. That's what gets you prepared for the great future God has in store.

Flourish

But I am like an olive tree flourishing in the house of God; I trust in God's unfailing love for ever and ever.

Psalm 52:8

The next time you go through a disappointment or a setback, or the medical report isn't good, you can be honest and say, "This stinks, but I know a secret. It's just fertilizer. It's going to cause me to bloom, to blossom, to flourish." When you see that person at work who gets on your nerves and doesn't treat you with respect, instead of getting upset, just smile and say to yourself, "You're just fertilizer. You stink, but you're helping me grow. You think you're pushing me down, but really you're pushing me up."

You may feel as though you got too much fertilizer. But if you got a lot of stinky things that you could complain about, it's because God has a big destiny in front of you. He's getting you prepared for blessings.

Rooted Deep

Let your roots grow down into him, and let your lives be built on him. Then your faith will grow strong in the truth you were taught...

Colossians 2:7 NLT

MAY 31

Joseph's brothers sold him into slavery in Egypt, where his master's wife falsely accused him of a crime and had him thrown into prison. He spent thirteen years there for something he didn't do. He could have gotten depressed and said, "God, this is unfair. I'm a good person." Instead he realized, "It's just fertilizer. They're trying to stop me, but God's going to use it to increase me." They didn't realize they were pouring fertilizer on him. Joseph kept growing, getting stronger, his roots going down deeper in faith. All that injustice, that stinky stuff, seemed like a waste of years of his life, but just as fertilizer feeds a plant nutrients and minerals, that difficult, dark season was doing a work in Joseph, getting him prepared for the fullness of his destiny.

The Final Say

"Come now, let us kill him and throw him into one of the pits. Then we will... see what will become of his dreams."

Genesis 37:20 ESV

Joseph went from the pit to the prison and all the way to the palace. You may feel that you're in the pits right now. Perhaps you've had some bad breaks, you're dealing with a sickness, you've lost a loved one, a dream died. But that pit is not the end of your story, and the prison is not your final chapter. Your destiny is the palace. God destined you to live a victorious life.

If you'll stay in faith when you're doing the right thing but the wrong things keep happening, your time will come to be promoted, to be blessed, to be vindicated, and all the forces of darkness cannot stop you. People don't have the final say; God has the final say. He will get you to where you're supposed to be.

Sing a New Song

*[God] also brought me up out of a horrible pit...
has put a new song in my mouth.*

Psalm 40:2–3 NKJV

You may be in the pit as David said he had been, but you need to get ready, because you're coming out. That depression is not the end, and that addiction is not the final chapter. The person who walked out on you is not the end. If they left you, you didn't need them. If they walked out, they were not a part of your destiny. God has somebody better. He wants to put a new song in your heart. Don't get comfortable in the pit. Don't let self-pity and discouragement steal your passion. Every blessing that God promised you He still has every intention of bringing to pass. Dreams coming to pass are in your future, with increase, abundance, promotion, health, and restoration. That's what's up in front of you. That's where your story ends.

Stay on the High Ground

*For the LORD will vindicate his people and
have compassion on his servants.*

Psalm 135:14

I talked to a man who was very upset because his boss was jealous of him and held him back from being promoted. I told him, "It's just fertilizer. Stay on the high road, and God will take care of your enemies. You're about to see new growth." This man got his passion back and went to the office being his best, working as unto God, not unto man. One day the company CEO heard this man give a report and was very impressed. About a year later, a position became available that would normally have gone to his boss, but the CEO offered this man the position. Now instead of his working for the boss, the boss is working for him! One touch of God's favor and you'll go from the back to the front.

It's Working for You

"I have seen his ways, and will heal him; I will also lead him, and restore comforts to him."

Isaiah 57:18 NKJV

Perhaps because of a mistake you made, you feel as though you're all washed up and have blown your chance. Remember that God uses the stinky stuff. You can't blossom into all you were created to be without some smelly stuff. It's not working against you; it's working for you. Sometimes we bring trouble on ourselves. We make poor decisions, and the accuser whispers in our ear, "You don't deserve to be blessed. It's your fault. God's not going to help you." But God doesn't waste anything. He knows how to get good out of every situation. It may not be good, but He can cause it to work for our good. Whatever brought the stinky stuff your way, you have to just see it as fertilizer. It's not going to stop you; it's going to promote you.

Turn It Around | JUNE 5

Then Jesus told her, "I AM the Messiah!"

John 4:26 NLT

The first person Jesus ever told that He was the Messiah was a Samaritan woman who had a rough past, had made many mistakes, and had gone through some stinky situations. God used her as the first evangelist to get the word out into her whole city that He was the Messiah. God took what the enemy had used against her—her boldness with men—and turned it around and said in effect, "That's gotten you into trouble in the past, but I'm going to use that to advance the kingdom."

God knows how to use what you've been through. He doesn't waste your experiences. You may have made poor choices, but He can turn your mess into your message. He'll use you to help others who are going through the same thing.

June 6

Nothing Is Wasted

"Let nothing be wasted."

John 6:12

A friend of mine was in an outlaw motorcycle gang, doing drugs, in and out of jail. One Sunday morning he was high on drugs and in such a dark place of depression that he decided to end his life. But he turned on the television, and there was my father ministering. This young man rode his motorcycle to Lakewood and was ushered right down to the front—leather jacket, tattoos, beard, mean as he could be. That day he felt a love he'd never felt and got down on his knees and said, "God, if You're real, help me to change. I'm giving my life to You." Today that man is a pastor of a church and has a motorcycle ministry. God doesn't waste what you've been through. He'll use you to help others who are dealing with the same thing.

Blessing Out of Dark Places

Who redeems your life from the pit, Who crowns you [lavishly] with lovingkindness and tender mercy.

Psalm 103:4 AMP

A young gunman walked into a school with an assault rifle and started shooting at police officers surrounding the building. After everyone scattered, he barricaded himself in a room where the school accountant had been hiding. Rather than panic, this lady got him to start talking. He told her how he was off his medicine and felt hopeless, as though his life had no purpose. She told him about how hopeless she had been, and how God had given her a new beginning and restored her life. She said, "If God did it for me, He can do it for you." The young man put the gun down and walked out peacefully, and nobody was harmed. Nothing is wasted—the good, the bad, the painful. God knows how to bring blessing out of the dark places.

Swords for Your Future

"Who is this uncircumcised Philistine that he should defy the armies of the living God?"

1 Samuel 17:26

First Samuel 21 records one of the times when David was on the run from King Saul and in desperate need of a weapon. He asked a priest if he had a sword or spear he could borrow. The priest happened to have the sword of Goliath. David left that day with the sword that had been meant to defeat him, and he used that same sword to defeat others.

You have some swords for your future—things you've overcome, battles you've won, enemies you've defeated, challenges you've outlasted. Those victories will be there when you need them. It was meant to stop you, but God knows how to not only turn it around, not only give you the victory, but put that sword in your future. That will help you overcome other obstacles.

Make Music

*"I will seek what was lost
and bring back what was
driven away, bind up the
broken and strengthen
what was sick."*

Ezekiel 34:16 NKJV

A small city in South America was built on
a garbage dump. The poor people who
live there make their living by going through
the trash, looking for anything they can sell.
But a man named Favio Chávez wanted to
help. He decided to start a music school
right there in the trash heap. He and a local
carpenter made instruments out of pieces
of trash. Then Chávez taught the children
how to play. Now they have what they call
the Recycled Orchestra and are invited to
play in packed concert halls around the
world. People started donating not only
new instruments but also funds to help the
children. That's what God does. He takes the
broken pieces of our lives—the mistakes, the
injustices, what seems like a waste—and He
makes music out of our mess.

His Mighty Hand

Humble yourselves, therefore, under God's mighty hand, that he may lift you up in due time.

1 Peter 5:6

You may be going through a tough time, but God is going to use what you've been through to catapult you forward. People can't stop it, bad breaks can't stop it, trash can't stop it, injustice can't stop it, and mistakes you've made don't have to stop it.

God has you in the palms of His hands. Nothing that's happened to you has been wasted. It's all a part of the plan to make you into who you were created to be. It may not have been good, but God can cause it to work out for your good. He can take the same thing that should have destroyed you and use it to propel you. The forces that are for you are greater than the forces that are against you.

Always in Blossom

You're a tree replanted in Eden, bearing fresh fruit every month, never dropping a leaf, always in blossom.

Psalm 1:3 MSG

JUNE 11

You may be in a dark pit, but you're about to rise to the top. Let go of what didn't work out, shake off the self-pity, the doubt, and the discouragement, for this a new day. God has new mountains for you to climb. Your best days are not your yesterdays; they are still out in front of you. The enemy wouldn't be fighting you this hard if he didn't know that God has something amazing in your future. It may be difficult, it may stink, but remember that it's fertilizer. It's working for you. You're growing, you're getting stronger. I believe and declare you're about to bloom, you're about to blossom, you're about to flourish. I speak victory over you, I speak restoration, and I speak new beginnings and blessings—health, wholeness, creativity, justice, vindication, and abundance!

Trouble Is Transportation

The LORD directs our steps, so why try to understand everything along the way?

Proverbs 20:24 NLT

We all go through things we don't understand, but God uses difficulties to move us toward our destiny. Nothing happens by accident. Looking back over my life, I see the importance of the times when I was most uncomfortable, when I went through a disappointment. It didn't make sense to me then, but years later I realized that if it had not happened, I would never have met a certain person or had the experience that I needed for a new challenge. If that door hadn't closed, a bigger door would never have opened.

Now I can see that the whole time, God was directing my steps. I thought I was going backward, but He was setting me up to move forward. The truth is that trouble was transportation; it was moving me into my destiny.

Through It All

*Many hardships and perplexing circumstances
confront the righteous, but the LORD
rescues him from them all.*

Psalm 34:19 AMP

You won't become all you were created to be without trouble. You don't grow in the good times; you grow in the tough times, the dark times. Trouble prepares you for the next level. Trouble develops something in you that you can't get when it's easy and everything is going your way. In the difficult times your spiritual muscles are developed, and you gain strength, endurance, and wisdom.

Every challenge you've been through has deposited something in you. Through every relationship that didn't work out, through those times when somebody did you wrong, you gained experience that will help you in the future. The times when you failed, when you blew it, weren't wasted—you gained insight. It was all a part of God's plan.

JUNE 14

You Are Extraordinary

God is our refuge and strength [mighty and impenetrable], a very present and well-proved help in trouble.

Psalm 46:1 AMP

When troubles come our way, it's easy to get discouraged. But God wouldn't have allowed it if it weren't going to work to your advantage. That's why you need to quit complaining and being discouraged because life dealt you a tough hand. The reason you have big challenges is that you have a big destiny. Average people have average problems; ordinary people have ordinary challenges. You're not average. You're a child of the Most High God. The Creator of the universe breathed His life into you. He crowned you with His favor. He put seeds of greatness on the inside. You're not ordinary; you're extraordinary. Don't be surprised if you face extraordinary challenges. It's because you have an extraordinary destiny. God is getting you prepared for greater blessings than you can imagine.

His Purpose Stands

"Devise your strategy, but it will be thwarted; propose your plan, but it will not stand, for God is with us."

Isaiah 8:10

Pharaoh's decree that the midwives should kill all the male Hebrew babies threatened the life of the baby Moses. Some would say that it was too bad he was born at the wrong time. Hidden in a basket among the reeds along the bank of the Nile River, Moses' life could have ended by a thousand things, but none of it was a surprise to God. None of it cancelled Moses' purpose. God has the final say. People don't determine your destiny; God does.

It just so happened that Pharaoh's daughter discovered the little basket floating among the reeds and was so thrilled with the Hebrew baby that she picked him up and said, "I'm going to take this baby as my own." And so Moses was raised in the palace of Pharaoh's daughter!

June 16

Part of His Plan

Your word, LORD, is eternal;
it stands firm in the heavens.

Psalm 119:89

God used Pharaoh's dark decree that threatened Moses' life to get Moses to where He wanted him to be. The trouble was a part of God's plan. If Moses had been raised in the limited environment he'd been born into, he could not have learned what he needed for his destiny. In the palace, he learned the best of Egyptian civilization—about business, leadership, how to speak to people, and on and on.

At the time that Moses was taken away from his home, I'm sure that his mother couldn't understand it. But many years later, when God told Moses to go back to Egypt and tell the Pharaoh, "Let My people go," Moses could walk into Pharaoh's court with confidence because he had lived in a palace and had been raised by royalty.

June 17

To the Next Level

*Blessed is the one who perseveres under trial
because, having stood the test, that person
will receive the crown of life...*

James 1:12

What was it that had prepared Moses to lead the Israelites out of Egypt? Trouble. It was being born in a dysfunctional situation, having the odds stacked against him. If Pharaoh had not put out the decree, Moses would have grown up in his own home, but as a slave with a limited education. As it was, he grew up in a royal environment and knew Egyptian protocol and wasn't overwhelmed by Pharaoh's court.

God knows what He's doing. You may not like the trouble, it may not be fair, you're uncomfortable, but that trouble is transportation. As it did for Moses, trouble is taking you to the next level of your destiny. It's getting you prepared. You wouldn't be who you are today without all the things you've been through.

Readied for Warfare

18

God did not lead them on the road through the Philistine country, though that was shorter. For God said, "If they face war, they might change their minds…"

Exodus 13:17

The Scripture says that God didn't lead the Israelites on the easiest route to the Promised Land because they were not ready for war. He had to toughen them up so they would be prepared for what He had in store. Don't get discouraged by the trouble and say, "God, why is this happening to me?" That trouble is not going to defeat you; it's going to promote you. It's not hindering you; it's preparing you. You may not see how it could work out, but God has a way through the darkness. He's already lined up the right people. As He had for Moses, He has a Pharaoh's daughter who will be there to be good to you. He has the breaks you need, the vindication, the funds, and the healing.

Trust at All Times

Those who trust in the LORD are like Mount Zion, which cannot be shaken but endures forever.

Psalm 125:1

Y ou trust God when everything is good, so why don't you trust Him in the times of trouble? Why don't you believe that even though you don't understand it, He's still directing your steps? You don't have to live feeling stressed out because you had a bad break or discouraged because you went through a disappointment. That trouble means you're on the way to your destiny. If you'll stay in faith, you'll see God begin to connect the dots. You'll see there was a reason that door closed and a reason you didn't get that promotion. God had something better in store. He was using that trouble to move you into your destiny.

It's Not the End

The LORD is close to the brokenhearted and saves those who are crushed in spirit.

Psalm 34:18

Mike Ilitch was a great high school baseball player who dreamed of playing for the Detroit Tigers and was given a four-year contract to play in their minor leagues in 1952. He was thrilled, worked hard, and kept getting better and better, but after three years a major knee injury forced him to quit playing. He was very disappointed. Everything he had worked so hard for suddenly came to an end. He started making pizzas in a friend's restaurant and got so good at it that he started his own pizza restaurant. People loved his pizza, and his restaurant, Little Caesars, was so successful that he opened another one and another and another. Yes, that knee injury was a big disappointment, but it wasn't the end. It was transportation; it moved him toward his destiny.

A Better Way

*"Be strong and courageous.
Do not be afraid or
terrified because of them,
for the LORD your God
goes with you..."*

Deuteronomy 31:6

My friend Mike Ilitch's dream of playing
for the Detroit Tigers never came to pass,
but today he owns the Detroit Tigers! His
dream didn't work out his way, but God had a
better way. A devastating knee injury led him
to start what became Little Caesars Pizza.

"Well, Joel, something like that would
never happen for me." How do you
know? Your story is not over. God is not
finished with you. That bad break, that
disappointment, that divorce is not your
final chapter. If you'll do as Mike did and
keep being your best, keep believing, keep
praying, keep honoring God, then trouble
won't be the end; it will be transportation.
It will move you toward the new thing God
has in store.

Enlarge Your Vision

*"Enlarge the place of your tent, stretch your
tent curtains wide, do not hold back."*

Isaiah 54:2

What you're dreaming about may be too small. That door may have closed because God has something bigger for you. You're working for a company, but one day you're going to own your own company. You're thinking you'll be single for the rest of your life, but God is going to bring somebody to you who is better than you imagined. That trouble is not the end.

I'm asking you to trust Him in the troubled times. Dare to believe that He's in control, that He knows what's best, that your steps and your stops are ordered by the Lord. It's a powerful attitude when you can say, "God, I trust You in trouble. I trust You when it's not happening my way. I trust You even though I feel as though I'm going backward."

With All Power

…being strengthened with all power according to his glorious might so that you may have great endurance and patience.

Colossians 1:11

A lot of times we're trying to pray away all our troubles, pray away the challenges, pray away the bad breaks. But here's the key: you're not anointed from trouble, you are anointed for trouble. The Scripture says, "God is a present help in trouble." He is not going to stop every difficulty and every bad break, but He will give you the strength, the power, and the grace to go through the dark times with a good attitude. In Psalm 89, God doesn't say, "I will anoint David so he doesn't have any opposition or problems." It says, "I'm anointing him for the trouble. His enemies will not get the best of him. I will push down his adversaries and defeat his haters. He will rise to power because of Me."

JUNE 24

Anointed for Trouble

"I have anointed [David] with my holy oil. I will steady him and make him strong. His enemies shall not outwit him... he will be great because of me."

Psalm 89:20–24 TLB

Quit telling yourself, "I can't take this trouble! It's too much." Have a new perspective. Right now, God is breathing in your direction, making you steady and strong. You don't have to feel stressed out because it's not happening your way. God will defeat your enemies. That sickness, that legal problem, that trouble at work will not get the best of you. Why? Because you're anointed for trouble. You are powerful, determined, favored. The Most High God says you will rise to power. That means you will see increase, promotion, healing, and blessing. The trouble is moving you to the next level of your destiny. You're going to see God begin to connect the dots in your life. It may not make sense now, but one day you're going to look back and see what God was doing in the darkness.

Made Ready

*"Be ready and
keep ready…"*

Ezekiel 38:7 ESV

A couple of years after Victoria and I were
married, we sold a house and moved to
a different place. Three months later, the
buyers of our house tried to sue us over the
plumbing. We had done nothing wrong, but
I was so nervous and worried about going
downtown to the courthouse and give my
deposition that it sickened me. When the
lawsuit was dropped, it seemed as though
that whole ordeal had been a waste of time
and money.

But sixteen years later, when we acquired
the Compaq Center, a company filed a
lawsuit to try to keep us from moving in.
This time I was confident, strong, and clear
in my deposition. God used the previous
lawsuit to get me prepared for a lawsuit that
would affect my destiny. I realize now that
trouble was transportation.

June 26

Step by Step

Righteousness goes before him and prepares the way for his steps.

Psalm 85:13

When Joseph was a teenager, God gave him a dream that he was destined for greatness, but before that dream came true, he went through a series of very dark places. There were many years when he did the right thing but the wrong thing happened. However, when you study Joseph's life, you can see how God connected the dots. Being thrown into the pit by his brothers led to being sold to a man named Potiphar in Egypt, which led to being falsely accused and put in prison. In prison he met the butler and the baker and interpreted their dreams, which led to interpreting Pharaoh's dream and being put in charge of the nation. If you left one step out, the others wouldn't work. Every step was divinely orchestrated and moving Joseph toward his destiny.

June 27

Keep Doing the Right Thing

"God is mighty…and firm in his purpose."

Job 36:5

As was true in Joseph's life, you have to believe that what looks like a disappointment, a betrayal, or a setback is all a part of God's plan. It's transportation. It's moving you little by little through the darkness into your destiny. God knows what He's doing. God knew that He was going to need somebody in charge in Egypt who would show favor to the Israelites. So years earlier, He'd started this plan to move Joseph into place. What looked like trouble was really the hand of God. Joseph's brothers took away his freedom but could not take away the calling on his life. What people take from you doesn't stop your purpose. Keep doing the right thing despite the trouble, and one day God is going to connect the dots for you just as He did for Joseph.

You Are En Route

*The righteous cry out,
and the LORD hears them;
he delivers them from all
their troubles.*

Psalm 34:17

God will deliver us from trouble, but consider it in different light. The post office picks up a package in New York, and drivers deliver it to California. *Deliver* means they transport it from one location to another. It may go through five different stops along the way before it is delivered. In the same way, right now God is delivering you from trouble. You're en route, the process has started, and there may be some stops along the way. But don't worry, you're not delivered yet. You're in debt, but God is delivering you into abundance. You're dealing with depression, but God is delivering you into joy. When those thoughts tell you, "This trouble is permanent. It's never going to change," just answer back, "No, I'm being delivered. This trouble is not going to stop me; it's going to transport me."

Restoration | JUNE

"But I will restore you to health and heal your wounds," declares the LORD.

Jeremiah 30:17

29

Victoria Arlen was eleven years old when her health suddenly deteriorated, and she ended up in the hospital in a vegetative state. Despite the devastating news, her family believed that God could restore her health. Two years later, she woke up on the inside and could hear the doctors and her family, and on Sundays she would hear us on the television talking about how God is our healer. Trapped in her motionless body, Victoria would say in her mind, *This is not how my story ends.* Three years after her body shut down, she was able to open her eyes and slowly learned how to speak, move, and eat again. Nearly ten years after going into a vegetative state, she took her first steps without assistance. Now she no longer needs the wheelchair or crutches.

He Will Bring You Out

...that person can pray to God and find favor with him, they will see God's face and shout for joy; he will restore them to full well-being.

Job 33:26

Yesterday's reading was a brief telling of Victoria Arlen difficult ten-year journey to restored health. This beautiful lady became one of the youngest on-air personalities for ESPN. She's also an actress, a model, and a motivational speaker. Friend, trouble is transportation. Victoria told me, "I wouldn't choose what happened to me, but I wouldn't change it." It was meant for harm, but God turned it around and used it for good. You may feel as though you're trapped in your circumstances, in an addiction, in mediocrity. You don't think you'll ever get out. But as was true for Victoria, that's not how your story ends. The God who brought her out is the God who's going to bring you out. That trouble is going to push you into a level of your destiny that you would never have experienced without it.

In All Things

And God is able to bless you abundantly, so that in all things at all times, having all that you need, you will abound in every good work.

2 Corinthians 9:8

Trouble is not going to stop you. You wouldn't choose what you've been through, but when you see how God turns it to your advantage and opens new doors, you'll say, "I wouldn't change it."

Shake off the self-pity, shake off the discouragement. You're anointed for that trouble. You may not understand what's happening. It may feel as though you're going in the wrong direction, but God is in control. That trouble is not going to get the best of you. It may look like a setback, but really it's a setup for God to do something greater. If you'll trust God in the trouble, that trouble is going to become transportation. God is going to open new doors, turn impossible situations around, and take you to the fullness of your destiny.

He Will Lift You Up

Arise, LORD! Lift up your hand, O God.
Do not forget the helpless.

Psalm 10:12

I met a man a while ago who had just been laid off after twenty-five years with his company. He had been a faithful employee, giving it his best, loyal as could be. He felt betrayed, alone, and forgotten, as though he'd been dropped. He's not alone in feeling that way. I have a friend whose father was killed in an accident when he was two years old, and all through school he thought, *Why does everybody else have a dad, but I don't?* There was an emptiness on the inside. He felt dropped as a little boy.

You may have been dropped, but the God we serve knows how to pick you back up. David said, "God lifted me out of a horrible pit, and set my feet upon a rock."

Your Story Doesn't End There

*Although my father and my mother have
abandoned me, yet the Lord will take me up
[adopt me as His child].*

Psalm 27:10 AMP

Sometimes other people's poor choices
have a negative effect on us. Maybe you
were raised in an unhealthy environment, and
now you're dealing with the same addictions,
same depression, and same anger that
surrounded you every day when you were a
child. Those things keep getting passed down
from generation to generation. Some people
were taken advantage of and mistreated; now
they deal with shame and guilt, feeling as
though they don't measure up. It wasn't their
fault. Somebody dropped them.

David was dropped by people coming
against him, by rejection, by disappointments,
and by his own failures, but God said, in
effect, "Don't worry, David, that drop is not
the end." In the same way, that bad break,
that failure, those people who did you wrong,
that sickness, that addiction, that chronic
pain is not the end of your story.

JULY

4

Get Ready for Double

"Because you got a double dose of trouble…, your inheritance in the land will be doubled and your joy go on forever."

Isaiah 61:7 MSG

If you have been dropped, you need to get ready. God's about to lift you. He's about to set you in a higher place. He's going to take you where you could not go on your own— to a new level, to new opportunities, to new friendships, to new health, to new joy, to new fulfillment. You're not going to come out the same. The Scripture talks about how God will pay you back double for the unfair things that happened.

God is a God of justice. He has seen every lonely night, every wrong that's been done, and every person who's ever harmed you. When you have a bad break and you get dropped, don't get discouraged or bitter. Get ready for double. Get ready for increase. Get ready for favor. Get ready for new levels.

He Will Take Action

"I have surely seen the oppression of My people… So I have come down to deliver them out of the hand of the Egyptians."

Exodus 3:7–8 NKJV

When the Israelites were being mistreated in slavery, God told them, "I'm coming down to make your wrongs right, to bring justice, and to pick you up." Did you notice what causes God to get off the throne, what causes the Creator of the universe to stop what He's doing and take action? When He sees you being mistreated, when He sees that injustice, He doesn't sit back and say, "Too bad." He says, "That's My son, that's My daughter, My most prized possession. They've been dropped, and now I have to get down there to do something about it." When God goes to work, all the forces of darkness cannot stop Him. He'll make your wrongs right, He'll pay you back for the trouble, and He'll get you to where you're supposed to be.

July 6

Never Forgotten

"See, I have engraved you on the palms of my hands."

Isaiah 49:16

We all get dropped in life. It's easy to feel alone and forgotten, as though you don't matter. But don't believe those lies. Every time God opens His hands, He sees your name. He's reminded of you. You may have had some bad breaks, some closed doors, some people who didn't do you right, but God hasn't forgotten about your dreams or the promises He's given you. He hasn't forgotten about that baby you've been longing to have, that healing, that wholeness, that freedom you need. Stay in faith. Life happens to all of us, and you may get dropped, but remember that it's only temporary. God sees it. He's not only going to lift you back up, but He's going to take you to a higher place of blessing. You're going to come out better than you were before.

July 7

Justice Is on Its Way

*GOD will never walk away from his people,
never desert his precious people. Rest assured
that justice is on its way…*

Psalm 94:14–15 MSG

Mephibosheth was destined to one day take the throne. But when he was five years old, his father, Jonathan, and grandfather King Saul were killed in a battle. In a panic his nurse picked him up and took off running as fast as she could to try to save the boy's life, but in her haste she dropped him. Both of his legs were broken, and he became crippled for the rest of his life. He'd done nothing wrong. Yet he had to pay the price for somebody else's mistake.

If you follow the rest of Mephibosheth's story, you see that God didn't say, "Boy, too bad you had bad breaks." Rather, He said, "Yes, you got dropped, but that bad break is not the end. I'm going to pay you back for what's happened."

JULY 8

It Didn't Go Unnoticed

But You, O LORD, are a shield for me, my glory and the One who lifts up my head.

Psalm 3:3 NKJV

In yesterday's reading, the nurse of Mephibosheth had good intentions, but she dropped him. Sometimes well-meaning people can drop us in life. They don't mean to hurt us, but perhaps they made a mistake and said or did something they shouldn't have. They were working hard, struggling to make ends meet, and they weren't there when we needed them. Or they had bad habits, addictions that were passed down to them, which they've now passed down to us. They weren't bad people, their hearts were for us, but they dropped us. Now we're crippled with low self-esteem, with addictions, with negativity, with depression.

But nothing goes unnoticed with our God. He is saying to us, "Yes, life hasn't treated you fairly, but it cannot keep you from your destiny. I'm coming to lift you up."

Royalty in Your Blood

"As one whom his mother comforts, so I will comfort you; and you will be comforted in Jerusalem."

Isaiah 66:13 AMP

Mephibosheth was the grandson of the king, had royalty in his blood, and was destined for the palace. But he ended up living in a place called Lo Debar, which was one of the poorest, most run-down cities of that day, a dark place. Year after year went by, and I'm sure he thought, *Everybody has forgotten about me. I used to have big dreams and was excited about life, but look at me now. I'm crippled and living in the slums. All because somebody dropped me. This will never change.*

But God saw the poverty and lack he was living in. God didn't just sit back and say, "Mephibosheth, your nurse really messed up your life." Rather, God said, "I haven't forgotten about you. I have a David and Jerusalem in your future. Just wait and see."

Favor Is Coming

David said, "Is there still anyone who is left of the house of Saul, that I may show him kindness for Jonathan's sake?"

2 Samuel 9:1 NKJV

One day after King David had established himself on the throne of Israel, he had a desire to show kindness to Saul's family. Why would David want to be good to the family of one of his enemies? That didn't make sense. But God was whispering in David's ear, putting a desire in him to be good to someone who had been dropped—namely, Mephibosheth.

You may feel stuck in a dark place, but God is going to whisper in someone's ear to be good to you. You don't deserve it, you won't earn it, and you couldn't make it happen on your own, but somebody will give you a good break and step up and solve the problem. Restoration is coming, promotion is coming, favor is coming, and new beginnings are coming.

Your Time Has Come

There is a season (a time appointed) for everything and a time for every delight and event or purpose under heaven.

Ecclesiastes 3:1 AMP

Mephibosheth had been hiding, living in the run-down city called Lo Debar, hoping that nobody would know he was related to King Saul. After all, Saul had not treated David right. Imagine what people thought when King David's officials came looking for this crippled man. The whole town was buzzing with excitement. When word finally reached Mephibosheth, I'm sure he thought, *Oh man, they found me. Now they're going to get rid of me.* The officials said, "Come with us right now. The king is summoning you."

God knows how to make things happen that we could never make happen. God is a God of justice. The King of the whole universe was saying, "No, your time has come. I am going to get you out of this dark place."

Just the Beginning

*Praise be to the LORD, the God of our ancestors,
who has put it into the king's heart to…*

Ezra 7:27

When David went out to meet Mephibosheth, I'm sure he was expecting to see a tall, strong, good-looking man who looked like his grandfather King Saul. Saul had looked like a king, had a presence that commanded respect, and walked as royalty. But when David saw the frail Mephibosheth, with his shriveled-up legs, I can imagine him asking his assistant, "Are you sure this is Saul's grandson?" David was puzzled and asked, "Mephibosheth?" His question clearly implied, "What happened to you?" Mephibosheth had fallen on his face on the ground and was too ashamed, too insecure, and too afraid to face David. He exclaimed, "Here is your servant!"

But God had put it into the heart of the king to be good to Mephibosheth, and rather than this being his ending, it really was his beginning.

Seated at the King's Table

*"Do not fear, for I will surely show you
kindness…and will restore to you all the
land of Saul your grandfather; and you shall
eat bread at my table continually."*

2 Samuel 9:7 NKJV

When Mephibosheth was brought before
King David, he was so afraid that he
was shaking, thinking it was the end. But
David said, "Mephibosheth, don't fear. From
now on you're going to live here in the palace
with me. I'm going to give you all the land
that belonged to your grandfather King Saul.
I'm going to give you a full staff that will
farm the land for you, and you will keep all
the profits. And you will always sit at my
table and have dinner with me—not over
with the staff, not with my assistants or with
the military leaders. You have a permanent
seat at the king's table."

You may have been dropped, but you
need to get ready, for there's a seat at the
King's table waiting for you.

14

Reign in Life

...all who will take God's gift of forgiveness and acquittal are kings of life because of this one man, Jesus Christ.

Romans 5:17 TLB

You have royal blood in your veins. The Most High God breathed His life into you. He's crowned you with favor and destined you to live in the palace. That is a place of blessing, a place of wholeness, a place of victory. Maybe you've had some bad breaks, but you're still royalty. You still have the DNA of Almighty God. It's payback time. There's a seat at the King's table with your name on it. People may have pushed you down, but God's going to push you up. Circumstances may have dropped you, but God is the glory and the lifter of your head. Things will happen for you that you couldn't make happen. The favor of God will open new doors, causing people to be good to you, paying you back for the unfair situations.

His Goodness Follows

JULY
15

Surely your goodness and love will follow me all the days of my life...

Psalm 23:6

What's interesting is that Mephibosheth was never healed. It may seem as though this isn't a good ending. But I've learned that if God doesn't remove the difficulty, if He doesn't totally turn it around, He will make it up to you. You may have lost a loved one; you can't bring that person back, but God can make the rest of your life so rewarding, so fulfilling, that it takes away the pain. Perhaps a person walked out of your life and broke your heart. God can bring somebody new into your life who's so loving, so appealing to you, that you won't even miss the person who left you. God knows how to pay you back. Seated at David's table, I think that all Mephibosheth could say was, "Thank You, Lord, for Your goodness!"

July 16

A Covenant of Love

*Know therefore that the LORD your God is God;
he is the faithful God, keeping his covenant
of love to a thousand generations…*

Deuteronomy 7:9

My sister Lisa and her husband, Kevin,
tried for many years to have a baby with
no success. She went through all the fertility
treatments, had a couple of surgeries, but
still no baby. Lisa felt as though she had been
dropped. But as was true for Mephibosheth,
if it doesn't turn out your way, God will make
it up to you. One day Lisa received a phone
call from a friend in another state who runs
a home for teenage girls. She said, "We have
a young lady who's about to have twins, and
something told me to call and see if you
and Kevin would be interested in adopting
them." They knew right then that those girls
were for them. A couple of years later, they
also adopted a baby boy. Now they have three
amazing teenagers, as happy as can be.

July 17

Overwhelmed with His Goodness

Oh, how abundant is your goodness, which you have stored up for those who fear you…

Psalm 31:19 ESV

God knows how to make it up to you for when you've felt dropped. Don't get bitter or wallow around in self-pity. God hasn't forgotten about you. When He pays you back, it will be bigger, better, and more rewarding than you can imagine. When God overwhelms you with His goodness, when He brings you out with double, you won't think about what you've lost, who hurt you, or what didn't work out. You won't complain about the disappointment. Rather you'll be saying, "Look what the Lord has done. He's amazed me with His goodness." You're so amazed that God remembered you, promoted you, brought the right people when you didn't think you could go on—all you can do is thank Him for what He's done.

When You Need Help

"I have made you and I will carry you; I will sustain you and I will rescue you."

Isaiah 46:4

When David summoned Mephibosheth to the palace, he couldn't get there on his own—he was carried to the palace. Each night at dinnertime, he was carried to the table. He was carried to his bed. You may think, *I can't accomplish my dreams. I'm broken. I have these addictions. I'm dealing with this sickness.* But when you can't do it on your own, God will always have somebody there to carry you. You're not alone, and you're not forgotten. God has you in the palms of His hands. He saw the times you've been dropped. You didn't go down by yourself, and you're not going to come up by yourself. God has people already lined up to carry you, to encourage you, to help you do what you could not do on your own.

What You Can't Carry

As the soldiers led him away,
they seized Simon from
Cyrene…and put the cross
on him and made him
carry it behind Jesus.

Luke 23:26

When Jesus was carrying the cross to Calvary, He collapsed under its weight. There was a man named Simon who stepped in and carried the cross the rest of the way. You don't have to be strong all the time. Even Jesus fell down under the weight of the cross. The good news is that there will always be somebody there to help you, to get you to where you need to be.

On the cross Jesus felt alone and abandoned, and He cried out, "My God, My God, why have You forsaken Me?" It looked as though that were the end and the darkness had won, but three days later, Jesus was sitting at the King's table, the victor, not the victim. The enemy never has the final say. God is a God of justice.

Beauty for Ashes

"...to give them beauty for ashes, the oil of joy for mourning, the garment of praise for the spirit of heaviness."

Isaiah 61:3 NKJV

When you don't have the strength to move forward on your own, God has the right people lined up to help you. He's going to keep working, restoring, promoting, and increasing you until He gets you to your seat at the King's table. You may have been dropped, but today you're being summoned by the King.

This is a new day. Maybe you don't have enough joy, there's not enough laughter, and you're letting your circumstances and pressures weigh you down. But I believe that God is breathing new life into your spirit. The sadness is leaving and gladness is coming. Heaviness is going and joy is on the way. Your life is going to be filled with laughter and happiness. The Scripture says you will have joy unspeakable and full of glory.

Great and Mighty Things

"Call to Me, and I will answer you, and show you great and mighty things, which you do not know."

Jeremiah 33:3 NKJV

JULY 21

Many years ago, a young man in South Korea who was lying on his deathbed from tuberculosis. He was a worshipper of other gods, but finally in desperation he cried out to any god that might hear him. A few hours later, a young college student felt what she described as an unexplainable love drawing her to that man's house. She knocked on the door, and his mother answered. The college student said, "I know you don't know me, but is there anything I can pray with you about?" The mother began to weep and told how her son was on his deathbed. The young lady went in and prayed for him. He gave his life to Christ. Long story short: God healed him, and today, Dr. David Yonggi Cho is the founding pastor of the largest church in the world.

Set You on High

*If you fully obey the LORD your God…
the LORD your God will set you high
above all the nations on earth.*

Deuteronomy 28:1

Friend, God hasn't forgotten about you. He's a God of justice. You may be dealing with a sickness, a loss, or a bad break. You may feel as though life has dropped you, but you need to get ready. God is about to pick you back up, and He is not just going to bring you out the same—He's going to set you on high and bring you out better. It's payback time. God is about to make some things up to you. He's lining up the right people to come find you with blessings, with favor. I believe that as Mephibosheth did, you're coming into the palace—a place of healing, a place of restoration, abundance, opportunity, and new levels. You're going to take your seat at the King's table and see the goodness of God in amazing ways.

Balancing the Books

"I will give them back everything they've lost. The last word is, I will have mercy on them."

Jeremiah 33:26 MSG

In accounting, the term *balancing the books* means making up for a loss. If an account has a deficit, when you balance the books, you have to first take all the losses, all the deficits, and total them up. Then you know how much you need to add to balance it. When the books are balanced, nobody can tell there's ever been a loss.

In the same way, God has promised that He will balance the books of our lives. We all go through things that put us at a deficit—a rough childhood, a friend who walks out on us, the loss of a loved one. If nothing changed, we would be out of balance. But God will add up all the losses, the disappointments, and the heartaches, and He will pay you back.

Rewarded Greatly

...do not cast away your confidence, which has great reward.

Hebrews 10:35 NKJV

In Hebrews 10, the writer notes that the people had endured a severe time of suffering and persecution. He encourages them by saying, in essence, "God is a just God. He will repay the compensation owed us. He will settle the cases of His people." God knows what you're owed. You may go through seasons when you're out of balance—you have a disappointment, a loss, someone does you wrong—but God is going to settle your case. He's seen every tear you've shed, every injustice, every dark place. You're not going to end up in the red—lonely, disappointed, at a disadvantage. That's all temporary. The Creator of the universe is adding up all the deficits and saying, "I'm about to balance your books." Compensation is coming, promotion is coming, vindication is coming, healing is coming, blessing is coming.

He Pays Attention | JULY

*"For I the LORD love justice…
I will faithfully give them
their recompense…"*

Isaiah 61:8 ESV

When I was growing up, for thirteen years we had church in a small run-down building that had been a feed store. Some people considered us second class and made fun of us, joking about our building. They were good people, but they dismissed us, saw us as less than. In their book, we were not up to par.

Fast-forward thirty years and God has given us the Compaq Center—the premier facility in our city, in the most prestigious part of town. That was God bringing justice. God pays attention. He's keeping track of who's trying to push you down, to discredit you, to make you look small. He knows who's talking behind your back. He's adding up all the deficits, and at the right time He's going to balance your books.

July 26

· · · · · · · · · · · · ·

Family Justice

He remembers his covenant forever, the promise
he made, for a thousand generations...

Psalm 105:8

God is going to pay you back not just for wrongs done to you, but also for injustices done to those who went before you. My father never saw the level of influence that God has blessed me with at Lakewood. I recognize that I'm reaping what he sowed. This is God balancing the books in our family. There are people in your family line who did the right thing but for whom the wrong thing happened. They served, gave, and honored God, but they didn't see total justice. Get ready, because God is not going to leave your family unbalanced. There will be times when you come into blessings that you didn't deserve, good breaks that you didn't work for, open doors that never should have opened. That was God paying your family back what it was owed.

July 27

Payback

And the LORD had given the people favor in the sight of the Egyptians, so that they granted them what they requested. Thus they plundered the Egyptians.

Exodus 12:36 NKJV

For ten generations the Israelites had been in slavery in Egypt. They were mistreated, taken advantage of, forced to work long hours. After 430 years, God delivered them from slavery. Just the fact that they were finally free and able to leave was a great miracle. But they didn't leave as broke, empty-handed slaves. They had worked all that time without being paid. God said, "All right, it's time to balance the books." On their way out, God caused them to have favor with the same people who had mistreated them. Suddenly their captors had a change of heart and gave them gold, silver, jewels, and clothing. The Israelites left the dark place of slavery behind, pushing wheelbarrows full of treasures. That was God balancing the books, paying them back for those 430 years.

He Will Fight for You

"The LORD will fight for you; you need only to be still."

Exodus 14:14

God sees every deficit, every wrong done to you and your family. He knows what you're owed. As with the Israelites, there will be a time when He says, "Enough is enough. It's time to balance the books." He's promised that He's going to compensate you. Quit worrying about who did you wrong, what you didn't get, who put you at a disadvantage, and who's not giving you the credit. God knows what happened, and He's saying, "It's payback time. You're coming out, and you won't be empty-handed, looked down upon, or seen as second class. You're coming out vindicated, promoted, respected, with abundance."

You'll receive favor that you don't deserve, with blessings chasing you down. That's the God of justice compensating you with what you're owed.

When Life Is Unfair

Yet the L<small>ORD</small> longs to be gracious to you; therefore he will rise up to show you compassion. For the L<small>ORD</small> is a God of justice.

Isaiah 30:18

A young man told me about how he was raised in a negative environment. His father hadn't ever been in his life, and his mother was never around. He didn't understand why he'd been dealt this hand in life. I told him that life may not be fair, but God is fair. He knows what you've been through, and He's going to make it up to you. But here's the key: you can't go around with a chip on your shoulder, thinking about what your mama and daddy didn't give you. God knows what they didn't give you. If you'll stay in faith, God will balance your books. He'll pay you back. God is a God of justice. If you didn't get much in a certain area, He'll give you more in another area to make up for it.

He Is Just

For God is not unjust. He will not forget how hard you have worked for him and how you have shown your love to him by caring for other believers.

Hebrews 6:10 NLT

JULY 30

You may feel as though you were shortchanged in life—you didn't have a good childhood, or you're dealing with a health issue, or your boss hasn't treated you fairly. The good news is, God sees what you're owed. He's keeping the records. He may not be able to give you another childhood or bring back a loved one whom you lost, but He can make the rest of your life so rewarding, so fulfilling, that you won't think about what didn't work out. Balancing the books means you're not living in a place of loss or deficit, always thinking about what you're lacking and how you're at a disadvantage.

You may be unbalanced right now, but the good news is, God is going to balance your books. Payback is coming.

A Place of No Loss

As your days, so shall your strength be.
Deuteronomy 33:25 NKJV

When my father went to be with the Lord in 1999, I lost one of my best friends. For the first year or so, I was unbalanced—that loss was heavy. But God has blessed me in so many other areas that I'm not living from a place of deficit. He brought new gifts out of me, opened up new doors, and caused things to fall into place. What was happening? He was balancing my books.

The hand you've been dealt may not be fair, but it's not a surprise to God. He already has a way to settle your case. Every time you're tempted to worry, just turn it around and thank Him that payback is on the way, thank Him that you're coming into a place of no loss.

He Delights in Justice

*For the LORD delights in justice and does
not abandon His saints (faithful ones);
they are preserved forever...*

Psalm 37:28 AMP

Maybe somebody walked out of a relationship with you and broke your heart. Don't give up on life, and don't go around bitter. God saw the hurt, and He feels your pain. It's not the end. Somebody better than you imagined is coming your way. Maybe a dream didn't work out or you received a medical report that wasn't good. In those dark times, you have to keep reminding yourself that God is a God of justice. He knows exactly what's going on. You're not going to live in a place of deficit. All through the day, just say, "Father, I want to thank You that You're balancing my books. Lord, I believe payback is coming, restoration is coming, healing is coming." That attitude of faith is what allows God to pay you back for what you're owed.

Exceedingly Abundantly

Now to Him who is able to do exceedingly abundantly above all that we ask or think, according to the power that works in us...

Ephesians 3:20 NKJV

One day out of the blue a husband told his wife of fourteen years that he was leaving her and the children for another woman. She was totally blindsided and didn't know what she was going to do or how she could provide for her children. A few weeks later, a former friend whom she hadn't talked to in twenty years contacted her and asked her if she would be interested in being her business partner. Their business took off, and today this lady is incredibly blessed. She has plenty to take care of her family.

God can make things happen that you could never make happen. You may have gone through a disappointment, a bad break, and maybe somebody didn't treat you right. Get ready. Payback is coming. Vindication is on the way.

Special Favor

When the LORD saw that Leah was not loved, he enabled her to conceive, but Rachel remained childless.

Genesis 29:31 NKJV

We previously considered a lady in the Old Testament named Leah. She and her sister, Rachel, were both married to Jacob. Rachel was far more beautiful, and Jacob didn't give Leah much time and attention. I'm sure that Leah felt as though she were not good enough, inferior, at a disadvantage. She hadn't gotten her sister's looks. Leah went on to have six sons and a daughter before Rachel was able to have a child. Having a son was a big deal back in those days. God was saying, "Leah, because your husband is not treating you right, because you didn't get beautiful looks like your sister, I'm going to balance your books and give you something that causes Jacob to notice you. I'm going to enable you to have children before your sister."

You Will Excel

Surely, LORD, you bless the righteous; you surround them with your favor as with a shield.

Psalm 5:12

God gives special favor to people at a disadvantage. You may feel as though someone else got all the good breaks— the good childhood, the good looks, the winning personality. Don't worry. Your time is coming. God has some advantages for you that will cause you to stand out. You're not going to live always in the shadow of somebody more talented, more beautiful, or more successful. God is going to cause you to shine. You're going to excel, you're going to be known, you're going to leave your mark. What you think you didn't get in looks, in personality, in education, or in your upbringing, God is going to make it up to you. You're not going to live in a deficit. He's going to balance your books.

August 5

God Takes It Personally

*She gave this name to the LORD who spoke to her:
"You are the God who sees me…"*

Genesis 16:13

Once when our daughter, Alexandra, was four years old, I bought her an ice cream cone. Outside the store, a little boy bumped into her, and she dropped it. He laughed and thought it was funny. She came straight over to me, knowing that I would make things right. We went back into the store and this time I said, "We're getting three scoops rather than one." That's the way God is when somebody does you wrong.

When people look down on you, dismiss you, and try to make you feel small, that doesn't go unnoticed. God sees every injustice, every wrong, every tear, every bad break. When somebody does you wrong, God takes it personally. You're His child. He goes to work much as we do as parents if somebody mistreats our children.

August 6

Great and Marvelous

*"Great and marvelous are your deeds,
Lord God Almighty. Just and true are
your ways, King of the nations."*

Revelation 15:3

Don't complain about the trouble; that
difficulty set you up for double. That
bad break and disappointment may look
like a setback, but really it was a setup for
God to show out in a new way. He's about
to balance some books. He's going to settle
your accounts.

When there are people in your life who
have been against you, some of them for
years, and have tried to hold you down,
make you look bad, discredit you—things
are about to change. God is going to cause
them to see you in a new light. He's going to
cause them to recognize His blessing on your
life to a point where they treat you with the
respect and honor you deserve.

A Day of Recognition

"Take your flocks and herds and be gone; and oh, give me a blessing as you go."

Exodus 12:32 TLB

When the Israelites were stuck in the darkness of slavery, Moses told Pharaoh again and again to let God's people go, but Pharaoh wouldn't listen. He didn't respect Moses. He dismissed Moses as second class. Every time Moses went back to tell him another plague was coming, Pharaoh didn't pay attention to him. What's interesting is that after the last plague, when Pharaoh finally decided to let the Hebrew people go, not only did the Egyptians give the Israelites their gold and silver, but Pharaoh said, "Moses, take all your flocks and herds and go, and ask your God to bless me also." Instead of making fun of Moses, instead of seeing him as not good enough, now Pharaoh recognized the hand of God on Moses. He saw the anointing and felt the power to where he asked Moses to bless him!

A Change of Heart

AUGUST

8

The king's heart is a stream of water in the hand of the LORD; he turns it wherever he will.

Proverbs 21:1 ESV

Part of God's balancing your books is that people who didn't respect you, who dismissed you, and who discredited you are going to have a change of heart and ask for your blessing. They're going to recognize the favor on your life. God knows how to change people. You don't have to play up to them, or try to convince them to like you, or let them control and manipulate you in order to try to win their favor. No, walk in your anointing. Run your own race, always honoring God with excellence and integrity. God will turn the hearts of those who are against you and who disrespected you the most to ask for your blessing. It may not happen overnight. It may take years, but God will balance your books.

Those Who Are Against You

When GOD approves of your life, even your enemies will end up shaking your hand.

Proverbs 16:7 MSG

I met a pastor who told me he had been our biggest critic and used to tell his congregation not to watch our services on television. But a couple of years ago he went through a major health crisis and had to give up his church. He didn't know if he was going to live through it. One night he came across our program, and he said that for the first time he really watched it closely. He said, "Joel, I haven't turned you off since. You helped me get through the most difficult time in my life." He gave me a big hug and said, "Will you pray for me?" When you honor God, one day your enemies will end up shaking your hand. God knows how to make the people who are against you need what you have.

Vindication Is Coming

As for me, I will be vindicated and will see your face; when I awake, I will be satisfied with seeing your likeness.

Psalm 17:15

In the Scripture, a man named Saul was the biggest enemy of the early church (see Acts 9). He went around having believers arrested and put in jail. Nobody was more opposed to the followers of Christ than him. Yet when Saul was at the point of his deepest need, God sent a Christian named Ananias to pray for Saul and speak to his need.

You may have people like Saul in your life who have been against you for years. They may not be that menacing or vocal, but they're condescending toward you and treat you as though you're less than. Don't worry. God is your vindicator. Keep taking the high road, keep doing the right thing, and one day they'll need what you have. They'll come to you asking for your help and blessing.

Be the Bigger Person

"Brother Saul, the Lord Jesus, who appeared to you on the road, has sent me so that you might regain your sight and be filled with the Holy Spirit."

Acts 9:17 NLT

When Ananias went and prayed for Saul, his biggest enemy, he did good to somebody who had spent years doing bad to his fellow believers. This is a test we all have to pass. Will you be good to that Saul in your life when he needs what you have? Will you show him favor even though he hasn't treated you right? If you want God to balance your books, you have to be the bigger person and bless those who have cursed you. In their time of need, don't withhold your help. Do good to those who persecute you. Ananias walked into the house and said, "Brother Saul." He called his main enemy a brother and treated him as his friend. After he prayed, Saul went on to become the apostle Paul, who wrote about half the books of the New Testament.

Wait for Him

The fear of human opinion disables;
trusting in God protects you from that.

Proverbs 29:25 MSG

When people come against us and say
things that are not true, it's easy to get
frustrated and try to straighten them out and
prove to them who we are. But don't waste
your emotional energy on them. Wait for
God to do it His way. He sees every injustice,
every negative word, and He's adding up all
the deficits, all the wrongs. At the right time,
He'll make things happen that you could
never make happen. He'll cause them to
need what you have.

Friend, your time is coming. You're
not going to live in a deficit. You may
have had some bad breaks, gone through
things you don't understand. Take heart.
The God of justice is saying, "It's payback
time." He's going to turn the darkest of
situations around.

AUGUST 13 | Faith in the Middle

Do not think it strange concerning the fiery trial which is to try you.

1 Peter 4:12 NKJV

It's easy to have faith at the start. When your baby is born, or you marry that beautiful girl, or you start a business, it's exciting. It's also easy to have faith at the end. When you can see the finish line, you've fought the good fight, and now the dream is in sight. The challenge is having faith in the middle— when it's taking longer than you thought, when you don't have the funds, when the medical report isn't good. In the middle is where most people lose the battle.

But God never promised that we would reach our destiny without opposition, without disappointments, without things we don't understand. Instead He says to not think it strange when these things come against us. It's all a part of the process of growing us up.

Persevere

You need to persevere so that when you have done the will of God, you will receive what he has promised.

Hebrews 10:36

I know you can have faith at the start—that's easy. I know you can have faith at the end. My question is, will you have faith in the middle? Will you have faith when it's not happening as you thought it would, when it feels as though you're going in the wrong direction and it's dark and difficult there, when every voice tells you to give up and says, "You must have heard God wrong." Don't believe those lies.

Nothing that's happened to you has stopped His plan for your life. He's not up in heaven scratching His head and thinking, *Oh man, I didn't see that one coming. That bad break threw Me off.* God is still on the throne. What He promised you, He still has every intention of bringing to pass.

You Have His Promise

Then Mary said, "Behold, I am the servant of the Lord; may it be done to me according to your word."

Luke 1:38 AMP

In the Scripture an angel appeared to a teenager named Mary and told her that she was going to be the mother of the Messiah, the Christ. She would have honor and be admired for generations to come. I'm sure Mary was excited. But I can hear Mary years later, saying, "God, You didn't tell me my son would be mistreated, betrayed, and mocked. You didn't tell me I would have to watch Him be crucified and die a painful death."

When God puts a dream in your heart, He'll show you the end. He'll give you the promise, but He won't show you the middle. If He told us all it would take for it to come to pass, we would talk ourselves out of it.

August 16

Stand Firm

Be on your guard; stand firm in the faith;
be courageous; be strong.

1 Corinthians 16:13

When God gives us a promise, as He did Mary regarding the birth of Jesus, He doesn't give us all the details. What you're going through may be difficult and doesn't make sense. This is where your faith has to kick in. Are you going to give up and talk yourself out of it? Or are you going to do as Mary did and say, "God, I don't understand this. You didn't tell me this person was going to do me wrong or that I would be dealing with this sickness. You didn't tell me this business was going to slow down. But I know You're still on the throne, and it's not a surprise to You. I'm not going to live in discouragement, give up on my dreams, or quit believing. I'm going to have faith in the middle."

Don't Get Discouraged

"Because the patriarchs were jealous of Joseph, they sold him as a slave into Egypt. But God was with him and rescued him from all his troubles."

Acts 7:9-10

God gave Joseph a dream about his future, planting a promise in his heart and showing him the end. What God didn't show him was the middle. Years later, when Joseph was ruling over the nation of Egypt, I can hear him saying, "God, You gave me this incredible promise, but You didn't tell me that I would be sold into slavery, falsely accused and put in prison."

If Joseph were here today, he would tell you, "Don't get discouraged in the middle. Don't give up when life doesn't make sense." You know the promise is in your heart. Keep believing, keep being your best. God hasn't failed you in the past, and He's not going to fail you in the future. Don't get discouraged by the process.

Fight the Good Fight

18

Fight the good fight for the true faith. Hold tightly to the eternal life to which God has called you…

1 Timothy 6:12 NLT

There are things that you're believing for—you know God has planted those seeds. The start is fun, and the end is exciting; but the truth is, the middle can be messy. In some way we're all in the middle; we're all on a journey. You know God gave you a promise, but every circumstance says just the opposite. Over time it's easy to give up and think, *There are too many obstacles to what I'm believing for. It's never going to happen.*

God has you reading this to breathe new life into your dreams. What He's placed in your heart is already en route. The process has already been started. The right people, the healing, the breakthrough, the new business is on the way. Now do your part and have faith for the middle.

Daily Readings from All Things Are Working for Your Good | 241

Believe the Promise

My eyes stay open through the watches of the night, that I may meditate on your promises.

Psalm 119:148

David could have said, "God, You promised me that I would be the king, but You didn't tell me that I would have to face a giant, or that King Saul would try to kill me, or that my own son would try to take the throne from me." When you study the heroes of faith, one common denominator you'll find is that they had faith in the middle. When it looked impossible, when the promise seemed far off, they kept moving forward, knowing it was a part of the process. They weren't discouraged by the trials or dark places. Yes, they had their moments. At times worry would come, fear would come, doubt would come, but they didn't allow it to stay. They stirred their faith back up and believed that the promise would happen.

Do Not Fear

"Do not fear, little flock, for it is your Father's good pleasure to give you the kingdom."

Luke 12:32 NKJV

When the Compaq Center was put on the real estate market, I knew it was supposed to be ours. God showed me the end. But He didn't show me the struggles we would go through to make it ours or that it was going to cost a hundred million dollars to renovate the center. Sometimes God leaves out certain details on purpose. If He had told me that I would be responsible for all that money, I would have settled for less than His best. If we had all the details, we wouldn't move into the fullness of our destiny because nobody likes adversity. We like to be comfortable. But you won't become all you were created to be without opposition, challenges, and difficulties that cause you to stretch and grow and use your spiritual muscles.

All along the Way

"He led them out of Egypt and performed wonders and signs in Egypt, at the Red Sea and for forty years in the wilderness."

Acts 7:36

When God brought the Israelites out of slavery, God showed them their destination, the Promised Land. He got them started on their way, but in the middle God didn't say, "I gave you the promise and now you're on your own. Good luck in the middle." All along the way God supernaturally provided them with blessings—parting the Red Seas, manna in the desert, water out of a rock, protection from enemy nations that were much bigger and more powerful. Again and again God made things happen that they could never have made happen. He was showing them and us, "I'm not just the God of the start, and I'm not just the God of the finish. I'm the God of the middle. I'm the God who will bring you through the trial, through the adversity, through the loss."

His Promises Never Fail

"Not one word has failed of all the good promises he gave through his servant Moses."

1 Kings 8:56

When you're in the middle, God has given you the promise, and you know the destination. But you're en route. You're in the process of raising your child, believing for your healing, or running that business. Along the way you'll face situations that look impossible—the odds are against you, the opposition is stronger, the report says you're not going to get well. Be encouraged, knowing that the God of the middle is right there with you. There may be a Red Sea in your path. It looks as though you're stuck, but the good news is, God knows how to part it. He can still bring water out of a rock. He can cause walls that have been stopping you to suddenly come tumbling down. Now do your part—have faith in the middle.

AUGUST

23

Through Deep Waters

"When you go through deep waters, I will be with you."

Isaiah 43:2 NLT

Y ou may be in deep waters today, but God is saying, "You're not staying there. You're going through it." When you're in the middle, you need to remind yourself that this too shall pass. It's temporary. Now quit putting so much energy into something that's not going to last. Quit wasting time by worrying about that situation at work, being upset over that medical report, or being frustrated with that person who did you wrong. The trouble is not permanent. The sickness, the loneliness, or the difficulty is just a stop along the way. But if you give in to it and let it overwhelm you with discouragement, you'll settle there and let what should have been temporary become permanent. This is where many people miss it—they settle in the middle. I'm asking you to keep moving forward.

Press Forward

I press on toward the goal to win the prize for which God has called me heavenward in Christ Jesus.

Philippians 3:14

David said, "I walk through the darkest valley" (Ps. 23:4). He didn't say, "I set up camp in the valley." He said, in effect, "The valley is not my home. I don't settle in the middle. I don't give up when it's hard, when life's not fair, when it's taking a long time. I have faith for the middle." When things come against you, and you're tempted to settle, you have to dig your heels in and say as David said, "God is the God of the middle. Even though I may not understand it, I'm not going to settle in the valley. I'm not going to get stuck in the middle. I'm going to keep moving forward, knowing that God is in control and this difficulty is just another step on the way to my destiny."

August 25

It's Not Up to You

The Lord will work out His plans for my life.

Psalm 138:8 TLB

The psalmist doesn't say that we have to work out our plans, make things happen with our own strength, and be frustrated when they're not happening the way we thought they would. We can stay in peace, knowing that the Lord, the God who created the universe, has promised He will work out His plans for our lives. Sometimes we know we should be going one way, but we're going just the opposite way. God knows what He's doing. His ways are better than our ways. Right now He's behind the scenes working out His plans for your life. He's arranging things in your favor, moving the wrong people out of the way, lining up the breaks you need. You may not see anything happening; you have to walk by faith and not by sight.

. . . .

Walk by Faith

For we walk by faith, not by sight.

2 Corinthians 5:7 NKJV

In the middle, Abraham could have said, "Sarah and I will never have a baby. We're way too old." But what Abraham couldn't see was that behind the scenes, God had already ordained a little baby named Isaac who had Abraham and Sarah's name on him. God already had it worked out for his life.

In the middle, David could have said, "I'll never take the throne. I'm a just a shepherd boy. I don't have the skills, the connections, or the training." But God is not dependent on what you don't have. When He breathed His life into you, He equipped you with everything you need. What you think you don't have enough of, the favor of God will make up for. The anointing on your life will take you further than people with more talent.

Open Doors

For a great and effective door has opened to me, and there are many adversaries.

1 Corinthians 16:9 NKJV

You may not be able to figure out how your dream can come to pass. The business plan tells you that you won't get out of debt until you're a hundred years old. The medical report says you won't get well. It doesn't look as though you can ever break the addiction. On your own, you're out of luck. The good news is that you're not on your own. You're not doing life by yourself. Your Heavenly Father, the Most High God, is working out His plan for your life. There may be obstacles that look insurmountable, but God has the final say. If you'll have faith in the middle, He'll open up doors that no man can shut. He'll turn situations around that look impossible. He'll take you further than you've ever imagined.

For Days of Trouble

Put on the full armor of God, so that when the day of evil comes, you may be able to stand your ground.

Ephesians 6:13

In life we'll all have days of trouble, days of darkness. But the same God who said there will be a day of trouble has also said there will be a day when that trouble comes to an end. You may be in difficulty right now. Be encouraged—it's not permanent, that trouble has an expiration date. God has set an end to it. You're in the middle now, but the end will come. Don't be overwhelmed by that sickness or situation in your finances—it has an expiration date. It's one of those days of trouble. Instead of being discouraged, remind yourself, "This trouble has an end date." It's not permanent. Just as there is a day of trouble, God has a day of deliverance, a day of healing, a day of abundance, a day of breakthrough.

A Day of Deliverance

Then they cried out to the LORD in their trouble, and he delivered them from their distress.

Psalm 107:6

A couple has a son who was addicted to drugs for over twenty years. Year after year, it didn't look as though anything was changing. They were in the valley, but they believed that just as there had been a day of trouble when their son got addicted, there would be a day of deliverance. They prayed, they believed, they sent him to rehab, but nothing worked. Then some people befriended the young man and paid his way through treatment, and for the first time in more than twenty years, he's completely free.

What happened? He came into his day of deliverance. What his parents couldn't do, God caused somebody to do for him. When you have faith in the middle, God will make things happen that you can't make happen.

You Will Prevail

"...no weapon forged against you will prevail, and you will refute every tongue that accuses you."

Isaiah 54:17

In Mark 4, Jesus said to His disciples, "Let's go to the other side of the lake," but along the way they were caught in a huge storm. The winds were so strong that the disciples thought the boat was going to capsize, so they woke Jesus up. He rebuked the storm and everything calmed down.

Why did He suggest going to the other side if He knew they were going into a major storm? Because He knew that in the middle there would be difficulties, but when He declares we're going to the other side, all the forces of darkness cannot stop Him from getting us there. When God puts a promise in your heart, He's not worried by the storms. He controls the universe. What He says will come to pass.

Why?

Then he asked them, "Why are you afraid?
Do you still have no faith?"

Mark 4:40 NLT

In yesterday's reading, if Jesus had thought they were in danger, He would have gotten up without the disciples having to wake Him up. He wasn't going to let them all drown. When we're in a storm, we often get upset and panic as the disciples did. "God, You have to help me! This medical report is bad. My finances aren't making it. My relationship is falling apart. God, I have big things coming against me!" The reason it doesn't feel as though God is waking up is not that He's ignoring you or that He's uninterested. It's that He knows you can handle it. He wouldn't have let it come your way if it were going to sink you. He wouldn't have allowed that difficulty if it were going to stop your destiny.

No Match for You

What, then, shall we say in response to these things?
If God is for us, who can be against us?

Romans 8:31

Quit being upset and losing sleep over troubles and situations you can handle. God is not ignoring your prayers. He knew there would be a storm before it arrived. He's not answering because He's growing you up. He's teaching you to have faith in the middle. If He comes running every time you have a difficulty, your spiritual muscles will never develop. You'll never really learn to trust Him. When you're calm despite what's coming against you, that's a sign of maturity. That's a sign that you've developed faith in the middle. If God has not turned it around yet, the winds are still blowing and the waves are still rocking, take it as a compliment. That means you can handle it. It's no match for you. You have the most powerful force in the universe on your side.

Eyes of Faith

Then the LORD opened the servant's eyes, and he looked and saw the hills full of horses and chariots of fire all around Elisha.

2 Kings 6:17

Years ago, our daughter, Alexandra, was singing in front of thousands of people when her microphone started cutting in and out, and she couldn't hear herself. Every voice told her, "Stop! Nobody can hear you!" But Victoria just keep nodding and saying to her, "Keep going. You're doing good!" Alexandra made it through the whole song because of her mother's reassurance that everything was going to be all right.

Sometimes in life the microphone doesn't work. You're in the middle of your song, but somebody walked away or the business didn't work out. Every voice tells you to give up. But if you'll look up through your eyes of faith, you'll see your Heavenly Father nodding, saying, "Keep going! I'm in control." The key is to just keep doing the right thing.

Pass through It

"When you walk through the fire of oppression, you will not be burned up; the flames will not consume you."

Isaiah 43:2 NLT

You can't control everything that happens to you in life. Just be your best and trust God to take care of the rest. He's not just the God of the start, not just the God of the finish; He's the God of the middle. He has you in the palms of His hands. Right now He's working out His plan for your life. Don't get discouraged by the process. You may be in the fire, but it's temporary. You're going to pass through it. If you'll have faith for the middle, I believe the God of the middle is going to protect you, provide for you, and favor you. You won't get stuck in the middle. He'll open doors that no man can shut and take you into the fullness of your destiny.

Anchored to Hope

We have this hope as an anchor for the soul,
firm and secure.

Hebrews 6:19

An anchor is usually a metal device that is attached to a ship or boat by a cable and cast overboard to hold the ship in a particular place. Once the captain puts the anchor down, he won't drift and end up where he doesn't want to be. He can relax, because he knows the anchor is down.

What's going to keep your soul in the right place, what's going to cause you to overcome challenges and reach your dreams, is being anchored to hope. That means that no matter what you face, no matter how long it's taking, you know God is still on the throne. When you are anchored to this hope, nothing can move you. The winds, the waves, and the dark storms of life may come, but you're not worried. You have your anchor down.

September 5

He Has a Way

*"The Spirit of the Lord is on me, because he…
has sent me to proclaim freedom for the prisoners
and…to set the oppressed free."*

Luke 4:18

You receive a bad medical report, which would get a lot of people upset and negative, but not you. You're anchored to hope. "I know that God is restoring health to me." You go through a loss or a disappointment, and your emotions are pulling you toward bitterness and depression. But there's something that's holding you back. Deep down you hear that voice saying, "Everything is going to be all right. God has beauty for these ashes." That's the anchor of hope. Maybe your dream looks impossible, and every voice says, "Give up! It's never going to happen." Most people would throw in the towel, but your attitude is anchored to this hope, *I may not see a way, but I know God has a way. He's opening doors that no man can shut. Favor is in my future.*

Keep Your Anchor Down

6

Through Him we also have access by faith into this [remarkable state of] grace in which we [firmly and safely and securely] stand.

Romans 5:2 AMP

I've learned that there will always be something trying to get us to pull up our anchor of hope—bad breaks, delays, disappointments, unanswered prayers. You have to make sure to keep your anchor down. If you pull it up, you'll drift over into doubt, discouragement, and self-pity. When you're anchored to hope, it's as though you're tied to it. You may have doubts that say, "This problem is never going to work out." But your faith will kick in. "No, I know the answer is already on the way." On paper, it may tell you that it will take you thirty years to get out of debt. You could accept it, but because you're anchored to hope, there's something in you that says, "I know that God can accelerate it. I know that explosive blessings are coming my way."

First Have Hope

Now faith is the substance of things hoped for, the evidence of things not seen.

Hebrews 11:1 NKJV

In tough times, when life doesn't make sense, when your prayers weren't answered, when it's taking longer than you thought it would, my question is, do you have your anchor of hope down? Do you have that hope, that expectancy that your dreams are coming to pass, that you're going to break that addiction, that your family is going to be restored? Or have you pulled up your anchor, and now you've drifted into doubt, mediocrity, not expecting anything good? Put your anchor back down. Scripture says, "Faith is the substance of things hoped for." You can't have faith if you don't first have hope. You have to believe that what God put in your heart will come to pass, that you will accomplish your dreams, that you'll meet the right people, that you'll live healthy and whole.

Hope in God

Why are you cast down, O my soul?...Hope in God, for I shall yet praise Him for the help of His countenance.

Psalm 42:5 NKJV

One time David felt overwhelmed by life. He was down and discouraged and stuck in a very dark place. But then he realized that he'd let his circumstances cause him to pull up his anchor of hope. He said, in effect, "I'm putting my anchor back down. I'm going to hope in the Lord."

You may not see any reason to be hopeful in your situation. You have to do as David did and hope in the Lord. Don't put your hope in your circumstances; they may not work out the way you want. Don't put your hope in people; they may let you down. Don't put your hope in your career; things may change. Put your hope in the Lord. When you have your hope in Him, the Scripture says you'll never be disappointed.

Prisoners of Hope

*Return to your fortress,
you prisoners of hope;…
I will restore twice as
much to you.*

Zechariah 9:12

SEPTEMBER 9

To be a "prisoner of hope" means you can't get away from it. You're anchored to it. You should be discouraged, but in spite of all that's come against you, you still believe that you're going to see your dream come to pass. That sickness may seem as though it's going to be the end of you. You could be worried, but you know nothing can snatch you out of God's hand. Your hope is not in the medicine, not in the treatment, not in the professionals, even though all those things are good and we're grateful for them. Your hope is in the Lord, in the God who breathed life into you. He's the God who makes blind eyes see. He's the God who healed my mother of terminal cancer. Keep your hope in the Lord.

Soar Like an Eagle

…those who hope in the L<small>ORD</small> will renew their strength. They will soar on wings like eagles; they will run and not grow weary…

Isaiah 40:31

When you find yourself being consumed by worry, full of doubt, thinking it's never going to work out, recognize what's happened. You've pulled your anchor of hope up. The good news is that you can put it back down. Quit dwelling on the negative thoughts: *You'll never get well. You'll never get out of debt.* Turn it around and say, "Father, I thank You that the answer is on the way for whatever I need."

You need not be overwhelmed by the size of the obstacles you are facing. Goliath looked stronger and more powerful, but like David, you have your hope in the Lord. You know that if God is for you, none will dare be against you. That's not just being positive; that's keeping your anchor down.

Hope On in Faith

*Even when there was no reason for hope,
Abraham kept hoping—believing that he would
become the father of many nations.*

Romans 4:18 NLT

When God gave Abraham a promise that he and his wife, Sarah, were going to have their "very own son" (see Gen. 15), she was seventy-five years old. It was impossible. It had never happened before. Abraham could have thought, *I must have heard God wrong.*

There may be many reasons your situation will never work out. But you have to do as Abraham did—against all hope, hope on in faith. Don't pull your anchor up. God is a supernatural God. Sarah was over ninety years old when she gave birth to a child. There were plenty of times when they were tempted to think, *It's never going to happen. We're too old.* If they would have believed those lies, they would have drifted into doubt and never seen the promise come to pass.

SEPTEMBER

12

Every Promise Fulfilled

"You know with all your heart and soul that not one of all the good promises the LORD your God gave you has failed. Every promise has been fulfilled…"

Joshua 23:14

Are you drifting into doubt, worry, and negativity? I'm asking you to put your anchor down. Get your hopes up. Just because that promise hasn't been fulfilled yet doesn't mean it's not going to happen. You may have had some bad breaks, but that doesn't mean you're not going to fulfill your destiny. Shake off the self-pity, shake off the disappointment. What God promised you, He's still going to bring to pass.

Don't let other people talk you out of what God put in your heart. Don't let them convince you to pull your anchor up. God didn't put the promise in them; He put the promise in you. That's why you can have faith when others think what you're believing for is far out. You can believe for it even though it seems impossible to them.

Brought to Completion

But let patience have its perfect work, that you may be perfect and complete, lacking nothing.

James 1:4 NKJV

When I became pastor at Lakewood, the head of our children's department had already been believing to have a baby for over twenty years. She and her husband had tried and tried and went through all the fertility treatments, with no success. Year after year went by. One day in a meeting she made a comment about "when I have my baby." She talked as though the baby were already on the way. She didn't say, "If I have a baby"; she said, "When I have my baby."

This young lady kept her anchor of hope down. Twenty-nine years after she started believing for a baby, she went to the doctor for a checkup. He said, "Congratulations, you're pregnant! And not with just one baby—you're pregnant with twins!" God always finishes what He starts.

September 14

No Drifting

We must pay the most careful attention, therefore, to what we have heard, so that we do not drift away.

Hebrews 2:1

When I was a young, I loved playing in the waves of the ocean. After a couple of hours, when I looked around for my towel, I realized I was a couple hundred yards down the beach from where I'd started. I didn't realize that that whole time I had been slowly drifting.

The Scripture describes hope as the anchor of our soul. It wouldn't say "anchor" unless there was a possibility of drifting. This is what happens in life. If we don't keep our anchor down and stay full of hope, then little by little we start drifting, getting negative and discouraged. "I don't think I'll ever have a baby. It's been so long." "I'll never get well." "I'll never meet the right person." The problem is that you don't have your anchor of hope down.

September 15

With No Doubting

But let him ask in faith, with no doubting,
for he who doubts is like a wave of the
sea driven and tossed by the wind.

James 1:6 NKJV

What's interesting is that when I was at the beach as a kid, it wasn't a big storm or huge waves that caused me to drift. It was just the normal movement of the ocean. If you don't have your anchor down, the normal currents of life will cause you to drift. To drift does not require a major sickness or a divorce; just everyday life will do it. Perhaps you don't realize it, but you have drifted into a dark place of doubt. You used to be excited about your dreams, but the passion is gone. Maybe you've drifted into bitterness because you had a bad break, a person did you wrong. The good news is that you can put that anchor of hope down and start believing again, start expecting His goodness and blessings.

Don't Be Moved

"None of these things move me; nor do I count my life dear to myself, so that I may finish my race with joy…"

Acts 20:24 NKJV

When you're anchored to hope, you may have negative circumstances, but you're not worried because you know that God is fighting your battles. You may not see how your dream can come to pass, but you don't give up. You know that God is behind the scenes arranging things in your favor. You may have a disappointment, but you don't get bitter. You know that weeping may endure for a night, but joy is coming in the morning.

Anchored to hope doesn't mean you won't have difficulties; it means that when those difficulties come, you won't drift. Nothing big or small will move you or cause you to pull up your anchor. Sure there will be waves, winds, and changing tides, but you're consistent—your hope is in the Lord.

Stir Up the Hope

Therefore I remind you to stir up the gift of God which is in you...

2 Timothy 1:6 NKJV

Life is too short for you to go through it drifting, feeling negative, discouraged, and passionless. Get your hopes back up. If you don't have an expectancy in your spirit that something good is coming, it will limit what God can do. You have to stir up the hope. If you don't, you'll drift into self-pity, worry, and discouragement. "Well, Joel, if God is good, why haven't my dreams come to pass?" Because you have an enemy who's trying to keep you from your destiny. But here's the key: the forces that are for you are greater than the forces that are against you. Don't let what happens to you cause you to pull up your anchor. If you'll keep your hope in the Lord, God will get you to where you're supposed to be.

Crowned with Favor

You have crowned him with glory and honor.

Psalm 8:5 NKJV

Being hopeful is about your soul being anchored to the right thing. If you're not anchored to hope, you'll become anchored to something else. You can become anchored to discouragement and see everything with a tainted perspective. Everything is sour. I know people who are anchored to bitterness. They're so focused on who hurt them and what wasn't fair that bitterness has poisoned their whole lives. You can become anchored to self-pity and go around with a chip on your shoulder, always thinking about how unfair life has been. Being anchored to any of those things is going to keep you from your destiny. It's time to cut that anchor and come over into hope. God didn't crown you with favor and give you a royal robe so you could go around anchored to doubt, fear, and bitterness.

Push Forward

"You come to me with a sword, with a spear, and with a javelin. But I come to you in the name of the LORD of hosts...whom you have defied."

1 Samuel 17:45 NKJV

SEPTEMBER 19

When you face difficulties, keep the right perspective. A difficulty is not there to defeat you; it's there to promote you. David could have looked at Goliath and thought, *Oh man, I'll never defeat him. He's twice my size.* If David had taken up his anchor of hope, we wouldn't be talking about him. Goliath wasn't sent to stop David; he was sent to promote David. What you're facing is not meant to hold you back; it's meant to push you forward. Instead of being negative and saying, "God, why is this happening? How is it ever going to work out?" stay anchored to hope. "God, I don't see a way, but my hope is in You. I know that You have it all figured out, and You'll get me to where I'm supposed to be."

Expect His Goodness

Hope deferred makes the heart sick.

Proverbs 13:12

If you don't have hope that a problem is going to turn around, hope that a dream is going to work out, or hope that the new house is in your future, then your heart, your spirit, is going to be sick. When you're not hopeful, positive, and expecting God's goodness, something is wrong on the inside. We all go through seasons in life when things aren't exciting. It's easy to have the blahs and lose our enthusiasm. That's part of the normal currents of life. Nobody lives on cloud nine with everything perfect and exciting every day. Part of the good fight of faith is to stay hopeful in the dry seasons. When it's taking a long time, keep a smile on your face and all through the day say, "Lord, thank You that You have good things in store."

Cut Some Lines

"Stop doubting and believe."

John 20:27

One time I was fishing with a friend and his dad, and the anchor to their boat got so caught on something that we couldn't get it up. All we could do was cut the line. The alternative was to be stuck out in the gulf.

If you've been anchored to discouragement, worry, or negativity for a long time, you may have to do as my friend's dad did and cut the line, so to speak. The enemy doesn't want you to be free. He doesn't want you to be anchored to hope. He wants you to go through life feeling sour, discouraged, and doubting. It's time to cut some lines. It's time to say, "This is a new day. I'm cutting those lines, and I'm anchoring myself to hope."

Make It Your Purpose

22

But as for me, I watch in hope for the LORD, I wait for God my Savior; my God will hear me.

Micah 7:7

Owen is seventeen years old, and one of his favorite things to do was play basketball. His dream was to get a scholarship to play in college. However, in 2014 he learned that he has a genetic disorder that can easily be fatal if it's not treated. When he was told that he could never play basketball again, Owen cried for thirty seconds, but then he told his dad, "I'm only thirteen. I can still become a coach, or a referee, or maybe even work for the NBA." He didn't cut the line to his anchor of hope because he knew that this wasn't a surprise to God. Then Owen wanted to help other kids like him, so he started having fund-raisers. In February 2016 he raised $140,000! Owen says, "You can make it your excuse, or you can make it your purpose."

Arise, Shine

"Arise, shine, for your light has come, and the glory of the LORD rises upon you."

Isaiah 60:1

When life throws you a curve, you have to have the right perspective when dark times linger. A bad break, a disappointment, a divorce, or a sickness can't stop you. You may have had some disappointments, and life may have dealt you a tough hand, but that cannot stop your destiny. The odds may be against you, but the Most High God is for you.

Keep hoping on in faith. You haven't seen your best days. God has you in the palms of His hands. It may have been meant for your harm, but He's going to use it for your good. If you'll stay anchored to hope, what is now your test will soon become your testimony. You will rise above every challenge, defeat every enemy, and become everything God created you to be.

September 24

Pushed into Our Purpose

Many are the plans in a person's heart,
but it is the LORD's purpose that prevails.

Proverbs 19:21

We don't always understand why certain things happen to us. Maybe a friend you thought would be with you for years suddenly moved away. Now you're having to find new friends. Or at work, you had all this favor, things were going great, but now there's conflict, everything is uphill, and you don't enjoy it.

Sometimes God will let us be uncomfortable for a dark, difficult period so He can bless us later on. He'll close a door, which we don't like, but later on He'll open a bigger door. God is not as concerned about our comfort as He is about our purpose. There are times when He will shake things up to force us to change. His goal is not to make our life miserable; He's pushing us into our purpose.

Get Moving

GOD, our God, spoke to us: "You've stayed long enough at this mountain. On your way now. Get moving."

Deuteronomy 1:6 MSG

Not every closed door is a bad thing. Not every time a person walks away from us is a tragedy. God knows we won't move forward without a push. When everything is going well, we don't want to stretch or to develop new skills. To step out into the unknown can be scary. What if it doesn't work out?

We may not like it, but if God had not shut that door, we would have been satisfied to stay where we were. God loves you too much to let you miss your destiny. You have too much potential, too much talent, too much in you for you to get stuck where you are. He'll put you in situations that make you stretch, make you grow, make you spread your wings.

As He Purposes It

The LORD Almighty has sworn, "Surely, as I have planned, so it will be, and as I have purposed, so it will happen."
Isaiah 14:24

None of the difficulties you've gone through or bad breaks you've experienced were meant to stop you. They were meant to push you, to stretch you, to mature you, to make you stronger. They deposited something inside you. It's made you into who you are today. You wouldn't be prepared for the new levels if you had not been through what you've been through. When you face a difficulty, something you don't understand, instead of being discouraged, instead of complaining, have a new perspective. *This is not here to defeat me; it's here to promote me. I may not like it, and I may be uncomfortable, but I know that God is using it to push me to a new level, to push me to greater influence, to push me into my purpose.*

Steps of Faith

But the LORD said to me, "Do not say, 'I am too young.' You must go to everyone I send you to and say whatever I command you."

Jeremiah 1:7

When I look back over my life, I can see the pivotal moments when I really grew were when I was pushed. At the time I didn't like it, and I wanted to stay where I was. I wouldn't have done it on my own. God had to shut the doors and force me to take steps of faith. He pushed me into my purpose.

Sometimes we're praying against the very thing that God has ordained, against what He set into motion. The enemy doesn't close every door. Sometimes God closes the door. If the door closed and you went through a disappointment, don't go around complaining. The closed door means you're about to be pushed into your purpose— you're about to see new growth, new talents, new opportunities.

Turning Points

But Moses said to God, "Who am I that I should go to Pharaoh and bring the Israelites out of Egypt?"

Exodus 3:11

When I was nineteen years old, I started a television ministry for my father at Lakewood, but I didn't have much training. We hired a seasoned television producer who taught me how to direct the cameras, what good lighting looks like, and how to edit. After one year, when he announced he was leaving, I thought that was the worst thing in the world that could happen. I prayed that God would change his mind, but He didn't.

His leaving was a turning point in my life. God used that to push me into my destiny. Even though I was uncomfortable, I learned I could do things I'd never thought I could do. It was the best thing for me. If God had answered my prayer, I wouldn't be who I am today.

Move Forward

"How long will you mourn for Saul, since I have rejected him…?"

1 Samuel 16:1

SEPTEMBER 29

The prophet Samuel spent years mentoring King Saul as a young man. When God told Samuel that He was going to take the throne away from Saul because of disobedience, Samuel was so discouraged that God finally had to say to him, "Quit weeping over what I've rejected." God told Samuel, "I've found a new man. His name is David, and I want you to go anoint him as the next king."

Notice the principle: if you'll quit being discouraged over who left, the right people will show up. But that won't happen if you keep complaining about the Sauls in your life and what didn't work out. When you accept what has happened and move forward, the Davids will show up. The people you need will be there for each season of your life.

Difficulties Bring a Push

*"I thought, 'Surely I shall die quietly in
my nest after a long, good life.'"*

Job 29:18 TLB

Job had his nest all fixed up, had his house
just as he wanted it, and had a successful
business. Things were going great. He was
finally comfortable, but what happened? God
stirred up his nest. God doesn't bring the
trouble, but He will allow difficulties to push
us into our destiny. Almost overnight Job
lost his health, his children, and his business.
If the story stopped there, it would be a sad
ending. But Job understood this principle.
In spite of all the difficulty, he said, "I know
my Redeemer lives." He was saying, "I know
God is still on the throne. This trouble is not
going to defeat me; it's going to push me."
In the end Job came out with twice what
he'd had before. God's dream for his life was
greater than he could imagine.

New Discoveries

*"So, get going. I'll be right there with you—
with your mouth! I'll be right there to
teach you what to say."*

Exodus 4:12 MSG

For seventeen years I did the television production at Lakewood. I thought that was how I would spend the rest of my life. I loved doing it. But in 1999 when my father went to be with the Lord, I knew that I was supposed to pastor the church, but I didn't think I could do it. I didn't have the training or the experience. That loss pushed me to discover new talents, pushed me into greater influence. Every time I've seen major growth in my life, it has involved adversity, loss, and disappointment.

You may be in a situation where you could easily be discouraged, but God is going to use that to your advantage. He's going to bring you out increased, promoted, stronger, wiser, and better than you were before.

Something New

"Well done, my good and faithful servant. You have been faithful in handling this small amount, so now I will give you many more responsibilities."

Matthew 25:21 NLT

It's easy to think that a loss is the end, but you'll discover that it's going to birth you into a new level of your destiny, just as loss has done for me. The disappointment, the persecution, or the betrayal may be painful, and you may not like it, but if you'll stay in faith, it's going to promote you. I wouldn't be where I am today if God had not taken the television production man away and pushed me when I was twenty years old. I wouldn't be leading the church today if He hadn't pushed me when my father died in 1999. That was difficult, but God doesn't waste the pain. The pain is a sign that you're about to birth something new. The greater the difficulty, the closer you are to the birth.

Start Again | OCTOBER

3

You have let me sink down deep in desperate problems. But you will bring me back... up from the depths of the earth.

Psalm 71:20 TLB

Steve Jobs was one of the most brilliant minds of our generation. At twenty-one years old, he cofounded Apple Computer. By the time he was twenty-three, he was incredibly successful and known around the world. But at thirty years old, after creating this global brand, he clashed with his board of directors and eventually was forced out of the company he'd started. He felt betrayed and wronged. But he went out and started another company that created something that Apple needed. It was so successful that Apple bought it and brought him back as Apple's CEO, and he is credited with revitalizing the company. He said, "Getting fired from Apple was the best thing that could have ever happened to me.... It freed me to enter one of the most creative periods of my life."

October 4

Lifted Higher

As an eagle stirs up its nest, hovers over its young,
spreading out its wings, taking them up,
carrying them on its wings…

Deuteronomy 32:11 NKJV

Moses said, "As an eagle stirs up its nest, so God will stir up His children." When things are stirring in your life, when things are uncomfortable and you don't get your way—a door closes, a friend betrays you—shake off the self-pity and get ready for new doors to open, for new opportunities, new skills, new friendships. Don't complain about who did you wrong. If it were going to keep you from your destiny, God would not have permitted it. Don't think, *Well, that's just my luck. I never get any good breaks.* Turn it around and say, "God, I know You're in control and You're stirring up things because You're about to open up new doors, You're about to take me to a higher level, You're about to push me into my purpose."

October 5

Wait Wisely

*Look carefully then how you walk,
not as unwise but as wise, making the
best use of the time…*

Ephesians 5:15–16 ESV

When Victoria was giving birth to our children, it was very painful. The greater the pain of the contractions, the closer she was to giving birth. At one point the doctor told her, "When you have a contraction, I want you to push." He didn't have her push until the birth canal was open and the baby was ready to come. They have to wait for the right time. In the same way, when you're being pushed, that means the door is open. Something new is coming— new levels, new influence, new growth. God wouldn't be pushing if the door were closed and nothing good were in store. When you're being pushed, don't be discouraged. Rather be encouraged; it's the right time. Get ready, for something good is coming your way.

Room to Grow

6

*"He brought me out
into a spacious place;
he rescued me because
he delighted in me."*

2 Samuel 22:20

The womb is a wonderful place for the development of a baby. But if he stays in the womb too long, instead of the womb being a blessing, it will be a burden. At a certain point it's too small and will keep him from his destiny and limit his potential. He has to get out.

It's the same principle with us: when things get tight, when we feel pressure, it's easy to think, *What's happening? It was so peaceful. I want to go back to how it was.* But if you stay in that protected place too long, it will keep you from becoming what you were created to be. If you're being pushed, you're about to tap into gifts and talents that you didn't know you had.

Enlarging
Your Path

*You enlarge the path
beneath me and make my
steps secure, so that my
feet will not slip.*

Psalm 18:36 AMP

I mentioned in a previous reading that when
my father resigned from a denominational
church he had pastored for many years, he
felt rejected and betrayed and devastated.
He thought, *I've given so much. God, why is
this happening?* But the fact is that God was
orchestrating it all. God knew my father
would never reach his full potential in that
limited environment. Had those people
never been against him, he would never have
fulfilled his destiny.

Don't get upset with the people who do
you wrong, betray you, or leave you out.
God uses people to push you to where you're
supposed to be. Without them you couldn't
fulfill your destiny. They may think they're
pushing you down, but what they don't realize
is that they're pushing you up.

Out of Your Comfort Zone

At that time a great persecution arose against the church...Then Philip went down to the city of Samaria and preached Christ to them.

Acts 8:1, 5 NKJV

This persecution forced Philip out of Jerusalem. He was pushed out of his comfort zone. What's interesting is that previously God had poured out His Spirit upon the believers in Jerusalem. The same God who showed them that great sign could have stopped the persecution, but it was for a purpose—a plan to push them into their destiny. It was in Samaria that Philip saw the greatest days of his ministry. If he had stayed in Jerusalem, he would never have reached his full potential.

Maybe you've been pushed out of Jerusalem, so to speak, through a bad break, a disappointment, a betrayal. Don't be discouraged. Jerusalem may have closed, but Samaria is about to open. God wouldn't be pushing you if He didn't already have a door open.

Move or Be Moved

The LORD turned to him and said, "Go in the strength you have and save Israel out of Midian's hand. Am I not sending you?"

Judges 6:14

OCTOBER 9

A friend of mine worked at a job and knew he had outgrown what he could do there, but he was afraid to take a step of faith. He is one of the nicest people you'll ever meet and a model employee. Then one he shocked me when he told me he had been fired. It was like saying, "Mother Teresa just robbed a bank!" But God loved him too much to let him stay in mediocrity. Today he is a vice president at a major company.

God knows how to get you out of your comfort zone. He opened the door; He can close the door. If we don't take the hint, He'll push us. That closed door is God pushing you. If it weren't going to work for your good, God wouldn't have allowed it.

Blown by Winds

*"Do not be afraid, Paul. You must
stand trial before Caesar..."*

Acts 27:24

When God told the apostle Paul that
he was going to stand before Caesar,
he was on a boat headed toward Rome and
they were in the middle of a huge storm.
The winds finally drove the ship aground,
and all who were aboard the ship had to
swim to a small island called Malta. It looked
as though Paul's plans hadn't worked out,
but that storm didn't stop God's plan; it was
a part of God's plan. It blew Paul into his
purpose. On that island the chief official's
father was very sick. Paul prayed for him,
and the man was healed. They brought other
sick people, and they too were healed. Paul
ended up sharing his faith with the people
on that whole island, and many came to
know the Lord.

Something More Rewarding

O my afflicted people, tempest-tossed and troubled,
I will rebuild you on a foundation of sapphires
and make the walls of your houses
from precious jewels.

Isaiah 54:11 TLB

Even though it looked like a bad break at the time, God used a violent storm to push the apostle Paul into his purpose. And He will use the winds of life that were meant to harm you to push you into your destiny. You may not understand, it may be uncomfortable, but keep the right attitude. That storm is not going to defeat you; it's going to promote you. The storm blew my father from a limited environment to a church that touched the world. It blew my friend from a job where he wasn't using his gifts to the vice presidency of a large company. You're being pushed for a reason. There's something bigger, something better, something more rewarding up in front of you.

OCTOBER
12

Coming Out Better

We are hard pressed on every side, but not crushed; perplexed, but not in despair.

2 Corinthians 4:8

When you feel pressured, when it's tight and you're being squeezed, that's because you're about to see a birth. Where you are is too small. The womb was good for a time and served its purpose, but now you're coming into a season of new growth, new opportunity, and new talents. You have to be willing to go through the process. Have the right perspective. Say, "This sickness is not going to stop me; it's pushing me, and I'm coming out better." "This trouble at work is not going to hold me back; it's pushing me." "The people who did me wrong can't stop my destiny. They meant it for harm, but they don't realize that God is using it for good. It's pushing me."

Only Believe | OCTOBER

13

But overhearing what they said, Jesus said to the ruler of the synagogue, "Do not fear, only believe."

Mark 5:36 ESV

Every storm you have gone through, every bad break, and every dark, lonely season deposited something on the inside. It pushed you to mature, pushed you to trust God in a greater way, pushed you to be more resilient and determined. Don't get discouraged by the process. Perhaps you are being pushed right now—you're being squeezed, pressured, and it feels uncomfortable. You need to get ready, you're about to see new birth. If you'll keep the right attitude, God is about to push you to a new level. He's going to push you into greater influence, greater strength, greater resources. You're coming into a new season of health, favor, abundance, promotion, and victory. Those winds that were meant to stop you are going to push you into your purpose.

Route Overview

"...along unfamiliar paths I will guide them;
I will turn the darkness into light before them
and make the rough places smooth."

Isaiah 42:16

When I type an address into my navigation system, the "Route Overview" option gives me all the details of my trip. You know where you're going, how long it's going to take, and what to expect. Knowing all the details makes us comfortable.

In a similar way, God has a route overview for your life. He knows your final destination and the best way to get you there. But God doesn't show you the route overview. He doesn't tell you how it's going to happen, how long it's going to take, where the funds are going to come from, or whom you're going to meet. He leads you one step at a time. If you'll trust Him and take that step into the unknown, He'll show you another step. Step-by-step, He'll lead you into your destiny.

Courageous Faith

By faith, Noah built a ship in the middle of dry land. He was warned about something he couldn't see, and acted on what he was told.

Hebrews 11:7 MSG

Most of us wouldn't have any problem with taking a step of faith—starting a business, going back to school, moving to a new location—if we knew where the money was coming from, how long it was going to take, and that the right people were going to be there for us. But here's the key: God doesn't give the details. He's not going to give you a blueprint for your whole life. If you had all the facts, you wouldn't need any faith. He's going to send you out not knowing everything. If you'll have the courage to step into the unknown and do what you know He's asking you to do, doors will open that you could never have opened, the right people will show up, you'll have the funds and any other resources you need.

The Light You Have

Your word is a lamp to my feet, a light to my path.

Psalm 119:105

"A lamp" implies you have enough light to see right in front of you. God is not giving you the light that shows your life for the next fifty years. It's more like when you're driving at night and with your low beam headlights you can only see a hundred feet in front of you. You don't stop driving because you can't see your final destination. You just keep going, seeing as much as the lights allow, knowing you'll eventually arrive at your destination.

My question is, will you take the next step that God gives you with the light you have? If you're waiting for all the details, you'll be waiting your whole life. We all want to be comfortable, but walking in God's perfect will is going to make you stretch, pray, and believe.

Step into the Unknown

"Be strong and courageous. Do not be afraid; do not be discouraged, for the LORD your God will be with you wherever you go."

Joshua 1:9

When you're walking in God's will, you're not going to be sure how it's all going to work out, but that is what will cause you to trust Him in a greater way. God is not interested only in the destination. He's teaching you along the way; He's getting you prepared and growing you up.

Are you going to be bold and step into the unknown? The unknown is where miracles happen, where you discover abilities that you never knew you had, where you'll accomplish more than you ever dreamed. Just because you don't have the details doesn't mean God doesn't have the details. He wouldn't be leading you there if He didn't have a purpose. He has the provision, He has the favor, and He has what you need to go to the next level.

Endure the Silence

OCTOBER 18

For God alone my soul waits in silence and quietly submits to Him, for my hope is from Him.

Psalm 62:5 AMP

One thing I like about my navigation system is that it gives me specific details. "Go 9.3 miles down this freeway and exit at…" It's all right in front of me to see. But God does not direct us that way. He'll tell you to go down a certain road. Then the first thing we do is ask for details. "How far?" No answer. "Where do You want me to turn?" No answer. "Who's going to meet me?" No answer. It would be so much easier if God would give us specifics. But that wouldn't take any faith. Can you endure the silence of not knowing everything? Will you trust God even though you don't have the details? Will you take that step of faith even though you're nervous, uncomfortable, and not sure how it's going to work out?

Be Bold

By faith Abraham, when called to go to a place he would later receive as his inheritance, obeyed and went, even though he did not know where he was going.

Hebrews 11:8

God told Abraham to pack up his household, leave his extended family behind, and head out to a land that He was going to give him as his inheritance. The only problem was that God didn't give him any details, meaning he didn't know where he was going. I can imagine Abraham telling his wife, Sarah, "Honey, we're going to move. God promised me He's taking us to a better land where we're going to be blessed in a new way." I hear Sarah saying, "That's so exciting! Where are we going?" Abraham answers, "I'm not sure. He didn't tell me." At that point, reality sets in for Sarah, who responds, "Well, Abraham, are you sure that God told you this?"

If you're going to step into the unknown, it's going to take boldness.

Provision for Every Step

LORD, I know that people's lives are not their own;
it is not for them to direct their steps.

Jeremiah 10:23

Stepping into the unknown is not always going to make sense. Your own thoughts will tell you, *You better play it safe. What if it doesn't work out?* But just because you don't have all the answers, and just because you're uncomfortable, doesn't mean you aren't supposed to step into the unknown. The psalmist said, "The steps of a good person are ordered by the Lord." If you'll take that step, not knowing all the details but trusting that God knows what He's doing, then each step of the way there will be provision, there will be favor, there will be protection. Yes, it's uncomfortable not knowing the details; and yes, you have to stretch, you have to pray, and you have to trust. But every step you'll not only have God's blessing; you'll also be growing and getting stronger.

Walk on Water

"Come," he said. Then Peter got down out of the boat, walked on the water and came toward Jesus.

Matthew 14:29

When Jesus came walking across the stormy sea in the darkness of night, Peter was the only disciple who had the courage to get out of the boat and walk on the water to Him. I can imagine the other disciples saying, "Peter, stay in here with us! It's too dangerous. You could drown." But when Jesus told him to come, Peter stepped out into the unknown and walked on the water. Yes, Peter also sank, but he did walk on the water. Although what is familiar is comfortable, it can become a curse rather than a blessing. Familiarity—what you're used to, how you were raised, the job you've had for years—can keep you from your destiny. Don't let your comfort keep you from getting out of the boat and becoming who you were created to be.

OCTOBER

22

Purpose before Comfort

The LORD had said to Abram, "Go from your country, your people and your father's household to the land I will show you."

Genesis 12:1

If Abraham had put his comfort above fulfilling his purpose, we wouldn't be talking about him. You can't play it safe your whole life and reach the fullness of your destiny. Don't let the what-ifs talk you out of it. "What if I fail? What if I don't have the funds? What if they say no?" You'll never know unless you try. What if you excel? What if you discover new gifts you didn't know you had? What if it leads you to more opportunities? "What if I get into this new relationship and I get hurt again?" What if you get into it and you're happier than you've ever been? When you come to the end of your life, will you have more regrets about the risks you took or about the risks you didn't take?

Not Knowing | OCTOBER

23

"And now, compelled by the Spirit, I am going to Jerusalem, not knowing what will happen to me there."

Acts 20:22

For every major victory and every significant accomplishment in my life, I've had to step into the unknown. When my father went to be with the Lord and I stepped up to pastor the church, every voice said, "Don't do it! You're going to get up there and look like a fool." I knew I was going in over my head, and I knew I didn't have the experience. But I also knew that when we are weak, God's power shows up the greatest. All I could see ahead was this much: "Joel, step up and pastor the church." If God had shown me all that we're doing today, I would have said, "No way. I can't do that." Sometimes the reason God doesn't tell us what's in our future is that He knows we can't handle it right then.

October 24

Beyond Your Imagination

*"No eye has seen, no ear has heard,
and no mind has imagined what God
has prepared for those who love him."*

1 Corinthians 2:9 NLT

What God has in store for you is going
to boggle your mind—the places
He's going to take you, the people you're
going to influence, the dreams you're going
to accomplish. It's going to be bigger than
you've imagined. You know where it is—it's
in the unknown, in what you can't see right
now, in what you don't feel qualified for, in
what looks way over your head. When you
have something in front of you that seems
too big and you don't think you have what
it takes to do it, that's God stretching you.
You've been on that step you're on for long
enough. You've passed that test, and now
the next step is coming—a new level of
favor, a new level of blessing, a new level of
influence, a new level of anointing.

Without Wavering

Let us hold fast the confession of our hope without wavering, for He who promised is faithful.

Hebrews 10:23 NKJV

I was driving to another city on a country road for about a hundred-mile stretch, and I noticed that as long as I was on the right path, the voice of my GPS was silent. I wished it would come on and say, "You're right on track." But she never said a thing until it was time to do something different. Sometimes God is silent. You don't hear Him saying anything. It's easy to think something must be wrong. He's not talking. But that means you're on the right course. Keep being your best with what you have. Keep stretching, praying, and believing. The next step is coming. You have to pass the test of being faithful where you are. That next step is going to be an increase step, a favor step, a healing step, a breakthrough step.

In That Moment

"As soon as the priests who carry the ark of the LORD… set foot in the Jordan, its waters flowing downstream will be cut off and stand up in a heap."

Joshua 3:13

When Joshua and the Israelites came to the Jordan River, there was no way for them to get across. God told Joshua to have the priests who were carrying the ark of the covenant step into the river; then the waters of the Jordan would part. I can imagine the priests saying, "Joshua, that doesn't make sense. We could drown in those dark waters." They got to the banks a few feet away and nothing happened. Thoughts started telling them, *What if it doesn't part? What if we get out there and can't get back?* They could have talked themselves out of it, but instead they dared to step into the unknown and in that moment the water upstream began piling up. It wasn't long till the riverbed was empty and they were able to walk across on dry land.

A Test of Faith

As soon as the priests who carried the ark reached the Jordan and their feet touched the water's edge, the water from upstream stopped flowing.

Joshua 3:15–16

Notice that the miracle happened along the way. We think, *God, when You part the river, I'll go.* God says, "Go, and I'll part the river." God will purposefully put us in situations where we can't do it on our own and it looks impossible—that's a test of our faith. If you'll step into the unknown, along the way you'll see miracles, doors will open that you couldn't open, and the right people will show up. God was showing them and us this principle: when you don't see how it can work out or where the funds are coming from, when every thought tells you to play it safe, but you take that step of faith and do what God has put in your heart, you're showing God that you trust Him. That's when Jordan Rivers will part.

Surpassing Greatness

And [so that you can know and understand] what is the immeasurable and unlimited and surpassing greatness of His power in and for us who believe...

Ephesians 1:19 AMPC

When we stepped into the unknown to acquire the Compaq Center, God provided one miracle after another and we got the building! A week later, however, a company filed a lawsuit to try to prevent us from moving in. We were told that it could be tied up in the courts for up to ten years. When the CEO of that opposing company eventually flew in from out of town, our lawyers told us it was a ploy to try to confuse things. But he said, "Joel, I watch you on television, and my son-in-law is a youth pastor. Let's work something out." Two days later, the lawsuit was dropped. When you go out not knowing where you're going, you'll see Jordan Rivers part, you'll see Compaq Centers fall into place, you'll see the surpassing greatness of God's favor.

Prepared for the Journey

The LORD your God has... has watched over your journey through this vast wilderness...and you have not lacked anything.

Deuteronomy 2:7

OCTOBER 29

When you're in the unknown, when you're stretching, praying, and believing, that's when you're really growing. The journey is more important than the destination. Why? Because if you're not prepared during the journey, if you don't learn what you're supposed to learn along the way, you won't be able to handle where God is taking you. When you have to stretch your faith, that is strengthening your spiritual muscles. God could have given us the Compaq Center in the first week we prayed, or at least the first month. That would have saved me a lot of stress, a lot of praying, and a lot of believing. Why did He wait three years? He was getting me prepared. I was learning to trust Him, my faith was being increased, and my character was being developed.

Even Our Mistakes

But this I call to mind, and therefore I have hope:
the steadfast love of the LORD never ceases;
his mercies never come to an end.

Lamentations 3:21–22 ESV

It's interesting that during the three years we were acquiring the Compaq Center, I didn't hear God say, "You're doing good, Joel. It's all going to work out." I had to believe that He was in control when He was silent. I didn't know if we would be successful, but I took my steps believing that I was doing what God wanted us to do.

Here's the thing: even if you make a mistake, God knows how to use it for your good. God would rather you take a step of faith and miss it every once in a while than play it safe all the time and never make a mistake. Sometimes the mistakes, the closed doors, and the times we miss it are parts of God's plan. They're preparing us for the next open door.

Called by God

Only let each person lead the life that the Lord has assigned to him, and to which God has called him.

1 Corinthians 7:17 ESV

When my father went to be with the Lord in 1999, my brother, Paul, felt led to leave his medical practice to help us pastor the church, but it didn't make sense to his mind. In the natural it looked as though he were making a mistake, but as Abraham did, Paul went out, not knowing how it was going to work out. All he knew was that first step: "Go help your family."

What Paul didn't know was how the ministry was going to grow or that God would open the door for him to do medical missions, when he'd thought he was giving up medicine completely. What he couldn't see was that it was all a part of God's plan. If he hadn't stepped out into the unknown, he wouldn't have reached the fullness of his destiny.

NOVEMBER 1

Such a Time as This

"And who knows but that you have come to your royal position for such a time as this?"

Esther 4:14

When God asked the young Jewish lady named Esther to step into the unknown, it meant putting her life on the line for her people. In response to her what-if questions, her uncle Mordecai said, "Who knows but that you have come to the kingdom for such a time as this?" God was saying, "Esther, if you don't do it, I'll find somebody else. But the problem is that you're going to miss your destiny." This opportunity was now or never. I love what Esther did. She rose up and said, "I will go before the king, which is against the law; and if I perish, I perish! But I will not let this moment pass." She stepped up, and not only did God give her favor with the king, but she saved her people and became one of the heroes of faith.

Be Courageous

"Be strong and courageous, and do the work. Do not be afraid or discouraged, for the LORD God, my God, is with you."

1 Chronicles 28:20

Like Esther in yesterday's reading, we all have opportunities that are not going to come our way again. When my father died and I had to make that choice to step up or play it safe, that was one of those now-or-never moments. When they come your way, don't let fear talk you out of it or the what-ifs keep you in your boat. Do as Esther did. Be bold, be courageous, and step into the unknown. You may not have all the details, and you may not see how it's going to work out, but along the way through the darkness you'll see miracles. If you'll do this, you'll step into a new level of favor, a new level of influence, a new level of anointing. You're going to rise higher, accomplish your dreams, and reach the fullness of your destiny.

November 3

After the Storm

"Your Father...sends rain on the just and on the unjust."

Matthew 5:45 NKJV

No matter how good a person you are, there's going to be some rain in your life. Being a person of faith doesn't exempt you from difficulties. Jesus told a parable about a wise man who built his house on a rock. This man honored God. Another man foolishly built his house on the sand. He didn't honor God. Then the rain descended, the floods came, and the winds blew and beat on the houses. What's interesting is that the same storm came to both people, the just and the unjust. But after the storm was over, the house built on the rock was still standing. The house built on the sand collapsed and was completely ruined. The difference is that when you honor God, the storms may come, but when it's all said and done, you'll still be standing.

November 4

Built on the Rock

"Therefore everyone who hears these words of mine and puts them into practice is like a wise man who built his house on the rock."

Matthew 7:24

It's true that the rain falls on the just and the unjust. If the story stopped there, you'd think that it doesn't make a difference whether we honor God or not. "The same thing happens to me that happens to everyone else." But that's not the end of the story. Jesus went on to tell that after the storm was over, the house built on the rock was still standing.

You may get knocked down, suffer a setback, and go through some dark, stormy times, but don't get discouraged or bitter—that's just a part of life. It rains on everybody. If you'll stay in faith, you have God's promise that when the smoke clears, when the dust settles, you won't be the victim, you'll be the victor. You'll still be standing.

Still Standing

Put on the full armor of God, so that you can take your stand against the devil's schemes.

Ephesians 6:11

All of us can look back and see things that should have defeated us. You may have gone through a divorce or a breakup that could have given you a nervous breakdown, but look at you—you're still standing, still happy, restored, and whole. You've been through some difficult, dark places, but you've also seen the goodness of God. You've seen Him lift you, restore you, heal you, and protect you. That's the goodness of God. When you have this history with God, and you remember what He's done, you don't get discouraged by every difficulty, you don't get upset when people talk negatively about you, and you don't fall apart when you have a disappointment. You know that God brought you through the darkness in the past, and He'll bring you through in the future.

Do Not Worry

"The LORD himself goes before you and will be with you; he will never leave you nor forsake you."

Deuteronomy 31:8

About a year after I took over as pastor from my father, I heard that a couple who had been longtime members was going to leave the church. They didn't like the direction I was taking it in. I was doing my best, and the last thing I wanted was to lose any members. I was tempted to get down and discouraged, but then something rose up in me. I thought to myself, *I made it through the death of my father. I went through my darkest hour and here I am, still standing. If I can make it through that, I can make it without that couple's being here.* I heard God saying right down in my heart, "Joel, don't worry. They may leave, but I'm not going to leave. When it's all said and done, you'll still be standing."

Get Back Up

No matter how many times you trip them up, God-loyal people don't stay down long; Soon they're up on their feet.

Proverbs 24:16 MSG

If you are going through a difficult time, you need to look back and remember what God has done. He made a way when you didn't see a way, and He opened doors that you could never have opened. He put you at the right place at the right time. He vindicated and restored you. He did it for you in the past, and He'll do it for you again. Your house is built on the rock. You have God's promise that no matter what comes your way, when the storm is over, you'll still be standing. You have the DNA of Almighty God. You may get knocked down, but you're not going to stay down. There's something in your DNA that says, "Get back up again. That's not where you belong. You're a child of the Most High God."

Bounce-back

He restores my soul.
Psalm 23:3 NKJV

During the hurricane in Houston in 2008, big trees, small trees, oaks, pines, elms, and magnolias—none of them could withstand the hurricane-force winds. There was only one type of tree that I noticed wasn't blown down—the palm tree. It's because God designed the palm tree to withstand the storms. Unlike most other trees, the palm tree is able to bend so it will not break. After the wind subsides, it stands right back up as it did before. Why is that? God put bounce-back in the palm tree.

You may go through a dark period, but don't get discouraged. At some point the winds will subside and just as with that palm tree, the bounce-back put in you by your Creator is going to cause you to stand right back up.

Like a Palm Tree

The righteous will flourish like a palm tree.

Psalm 92:12

Today's verse could have said that we'd flourish like a strong oak tree or a tall pine tree. The reason God said we'd flourish like a palm tree is that God knew we would go through difficult times. He knew things would try to push us down and keep us from our destiny, so He said, "I'm going to make you like a palm tree with bounce-back in your spirit. You may go through a dark period of loneliness, of loss, of disappointment. The rain will come, but don't believe the lies that it's permanent. Don't believe that you'll never get well, never overcome the addiction, or never get out of the legal situation. No, you may be bent over right now, you may have some difficulties, but when the storm is over, you'll still be standing.

Strengthened

*"I will strengthen them in the L*ORD *and in his name they will live securely," declares the L*ORD.

Zechariah 10:12

What's interesting is that when the palm tree is bent over during the hurricane, you would think that's damaging the tree and making it weaker, but research shows just the opposite. When it's being pushed and stretched by the strong winds, that's strengthening the root system and giving it new opportunities for growth. After the storm, when the palm tree straightens back up, it's actually stronger than it was before. When you come out of the storm, when you straighten back up, you're not going to be the same. You're going to be stronger, healthier, wiser, better off, and ready for new growth. God never brings you out the same. He makes the enemy pay for bringing the times of darkness and trouble. You're not only going to still be standing; you're going to be standing stronger.

NOVEMBER 11 | Our Stronghold

*The LORD is the stronghold
of my life—of whom shall I
be afraid?*

Psalm 27:1

I have a friend who's had cancer three
times over the past ten years. Every time
it looks as though it's over, like a bent-over
palm tree, somehow he bounces back. He
knows that the number of his days, God
will fulfill. When the doctors told him they
were going to harvest his white blood cells
in two months to help restore his immune
system after chemotherapy, they gave him
a number of cells needed. He said, "I'll give
you twice that." Every day he thanked God
that he was getting better, and he went out
and exercised, did everything he could. Two
months later, he went back to the hospital,
and the doctors said, "You gave us more
than twice the number of white blood cells
we were hoping for." Today he's cancer-free,
having beaten it for the third time.

Revived

Though I walk in the midst of trouble, You will revive me.

Psalm 138:7 NKJV

Like a palm tree, no matter how hard the winds blow in your life, you cannot be uprooted, you cannot be toppled, you cannot be broken. Sickness doesn't determine your destiny; God does. He's the one who breathed life into you. If it's not your time to go, you're not going to go. God has the final say, and He said, "No weapon formed against you will prosper." He said, "A good man may fall seven times, but the Lord will raise him up." That's the bounce-back.

Now you have to get in agreement with God. He said, "Many are the afflictions of the righteous, but the Lord delivers us out of them all." The good news is, because you're the righteous, you have bounce-back on the inside.

November 13

Keep the Faith

I have fought the good fight, I have finished the race, I have kept the faith.

2 Timothy 4:7

It's easy to have a weak, defeated mentality that says, "Why did this happen to me? I don't understand it." It happened because you're alive—it's just a part of life. It rains on all of us. Your attitude has to be that no matter how hard those winds blow, they cannot defeat you. If you'll stay in faith, you'll be able to say, "Sickness knocked me down, but I came right back up. I went through a slow season at work, had some bad breaks, but it didn't defeat me. I came out promoted and stronger. I'm still standing." You'll be able to say, "Somebody walked out on me and caused me heartache and pain. I didn't think I'd ever be happy again, but look what the Lord has done. He brought somebody better into my life."

November 14

Rescued

So you see, the Lord knows how to rescue godly people from their trials…

2 Peter 2:9 NLT

I met a young couple who had moved to Houston from New Orleans, having lost *everything* during Hurricane Katrina. When I first saw them, it was as though they were numb. Their whole world had fallen apart. I told them what I'm telling you. "You may be down right now, but you have bounce-back in your spirit. When it's all said and done, you'll still be standing, stronger, healthier, and better." Week after week, they kept coming to Lakewood, hearing about how what's meant for our harm God will use to our advantage. A couple of years later, they brought pictures of the beautiful new house they had just bought. The man told how he had a better job, with better benefits. Their kids were in better schools. You may go through some storms, but there's bounce-back in your DNA.

Help Is on the Way

15

When the enemy comes in like a flood, the Spirit of the LORD will lift up a standard against him.

Isaiah 59:19 NKJV

You may feel overwhelmed—you lost your house in a hurricane, you got a bad medical report, a relationship went sour, somebody cheated you in a business deal. What does God do when the enemy comes in like this? Does He sit back and say, "Too bad. I told you it was going to rain. I told you that you're going to have difficulties"? No, Scripture says, "When the enemy comes in like a flood, the Spirit of the Lord will raise up a barrier." In other words, the difficulties, the injustices, and the sicknesses get God's attention. He goes to work just as we do as parents when we see our child in trouble, perhaps because someone is mistreating them. Like us, He doesn't think twice about stopping what He's doing and going to help.

Our Defender

16

> *But the LORD is with me*
> *like a mighty warrior;*
> *so my persecutors will*
> *stumble and not prevail.*
>
> Jeremiah 20:11

When our son, Jonathan, was about two years old, we were in a grocery store. As I was looking for something, he started pulling a few boxes of cereal off a bottom shelf. It was no big deal. I was going to put them back. But a lady who worked there came around the corner and nearly yelled with an angry tone, "Young man, you cannot take these boxes off the shelf!" When I heard that, something rose up in me. I'm nice, but if you mess with my children, I turn into the Incredible Hulk.

That's the way God is. When the enemy comes against us, God steps up and says, "Hey, wait a minute! That's My child. If you're going to mess with them, you have to first mess with Me."

Like a Champion

The LORD will march
out like a champion,
like a warrior he will
stir up his zeal…

Isaiah 42:13

In the tough dark times, you have to realize that you're not alone. The Most High God is fighting for you. He's got your back. He's brought you through in the past, and He's going to bring you through in the future. God looks at your enemies and says, "You want some of this? Go ahead and make My day!"

Now you have to do your part and get your fire back. You can't sit around in self-pity and think about what you lost, who hurt you, and how unfair it was. That's going to keep you down. Shake off that weak, defeated, *Why did this happen to me?* mentality and have a warrior mentality. A warrior doesn't complain about opposition; a warrior loves a good fight. It fires him up.

Out of the Ashes

David felt strengthened and encouraged in the LORD his God.

1 Samuel 30:6 AMP

NOVEMBER 18

When David and his six hundred men returned and found their houses burned, their belongings stolen, and all the women and children had been taken captive, they sat down among the ashes and wept until they could weep no more. It was David's greatest defeat. He was deeply distressed, and there was talk among his men of stoning him. It looked as though it was over, and it would have stayed that way if it had not been for David. Instead of his staying in the ashes, he reminded himself of who he was and Whose he was. He told his men, "We're going to go get what belongs to us." They went out, defeated their enemies, and got all their possessions back, as well as their wives and children. David's greatest defeat turned into his greatest victory.

Mighty Warrior

"The LORD is with you, mighty warrior."

Judges 6:12

We all face unfair situations. We may find ourselves in dark places, such as David experienced in yesterday's reading, that look as though we're going to be buried. But if you'll have this warrior mentality, if you'll stir your faith up and go after what belongs to you, the enemy won't have the last laugh; you will. He may hit you with his best shot, but his best will never be enough. You have bounce-back in your spirit. The forces that are for you are greater than the forces that are against you. Like David, you may be down for a season, and it may pour rain and flood, but because your house is built on the rock, because you have this warrior mentality, when it's all said and done, you'll still be standing.

Battle On

For our struggle is not against flesh and blood,
but against the rulers, against the authorities,
against the powers of this dark world...

Ephesians 6:12

One time I was lifting weights at home, lying on a bench, doing the bench press. By my standards I had a lot of weight on the barbell. I was doing my last set of five repetitions when I couldn't make the final lift, and the safety rails were out of place. Now I had all the weight on my chest, and I was totally out of energy. The weight was crushing me, and I ended up pushing on the right side with all my might and scooting over about an inch at a time until I was able to fall off the bench.

My point is that when you're in a tough time, you can either let it crush you, or you can push, scoot, squirm, stretch, wiggle, get your second wind, and beat it!

Strength for the Battle

You have armed me with strength for the battle.

Psalm 18:39 NKJV

I've found that the more difficult the battle, the more strength you'll have. Your strength will always match what you're up against. From yesterday's reading, when I think about how I got out from under that heavy barbell, I don't know how I did it. I had exhausted all my strength trying to finish the fifth rep. I could have said, "God, just take this off me. It's going to kill me." God said, "Push again and watch what will happen." I pushed and discovered strength that I hadn't known I had. Are you letting something defeat you because you don't think you have the strength to endure, the strength to overcome, the strength to deal with that sickness, that financial difficulty? If you'll have a warrior spirit and start doing what you can, God will help you do what you can't.

Resurrection Power

But if the Spirit of Him who raised Jesus from the dead dwells in you, He…will also give life to your mortal bodies through His Spirit…

Romans 8:11 NKJV

I saw a story on television news about a man who came up to a car that had crashed on the freeway. There was a person trapped inside, and the car had caught on fire. The man, who was about my size, grabbed the top of the door frame and somehow ripped the door away from the car so the trapped person could get out. They showed a picture of the steel frame, which looked like something a movie superhero had bent. They asked the man how he'd done it. He said, "I don't know. I just pulled as hard as I could."

When you do what you have to do, you'll discover strength that you didn't know you had. You are not weak or defeated; you are a warrior. You have resurrection power on the inside.

November 23

With Great Joy

*To him who is able to keep you from stumbling
and to present you before his glorious presence
without fault and with great joy...*

Jude 24

You may be down right now, those winds are blowing, but like the bent-over palm tree, you're about to come back up again, better off—stronger, healthier, and promoted. This is a new day. Things are changing in your favor. God has done it in the past, and He's going to do it in the future. You need to get ready, there's a bounce-back coming. You're going to bounce back from sickness, bounce back from depression, bounce back from bad breaks, bounce back from loss. Those winds can't uproot or topple you. The enemy doesn't have the final say; God does. He says that because your house is built on the rock, when it's all said and done, when the dark storm passes and the floods and winds subside, you'll still be standing, not the victim but the victor!

Remember Your Dream

*Praise the L*ORD*, my soul, and forget not
all his benefits—who forgives all your sins
and heals all your diseases.*

Psalm 103:2–3

All of us have things we're believing for.
Deep down we know they're a part of our
destiny, but then we hit some setbacks. Life
has a way of pushing our dreams down. They
can become buried under discouragement,
past mistakes, rejection, divorce, failure,
and negative voices. It's easy to settle for
mediocrity when we have all this potential
buried inside. But just because you gave up
doesn't mean God gave up. Your dream may
be buried in a dark place, but the good news
is, it's still alive. It's not too late to see it come
to pass. Instead of remembering the hurts,
the failures, and what didn't work out, the
key to reaching your destiny is to remember
your dream. Remember what God promised
you. Remember what He whispered to you
in the middle of the night.

Suddenly

Delight yourself also in the Lord, and He will give you the desires and secret petitions of your heart.

Psalm 37:4 AMPC

You may not have told anybody else about your dreams. They may seem impossible. Every voice tells you they're not going to happen. You've pushed them down, but God is saying, "What I've promised you, I'm still going to do. I spoke it and put it in your heart. It may not have happened yet, but it's on the way." If you'll start believing again, get your passion back, stir your faith up, God is going to resurrect what you thought was dead. You may have tried and failed, and it was so long ago, but dreams that you've given up on are going to suddenly come back to life. What should have taken years to restore, God is going to give you in a fraction of the time. He has the final say. He hasn't changed His mind.

It's Not Too Late

*Surely the arm of the LORD is
not too short to save, nor his
ear too dull to hear.*

Isaiah 59:1

You may not understand why something happened. You were doing the right thing, but the wrong thing happened. It's all a part of the process. Every unfair situation, every delay, and every closed door is not a setback; it's a setup for God to get you to where He wants you to be. It may be taking a long time, but all it takes is one touch of God's favor.

Why are you remembering the hurt, the disappointment, and the times it didn't work out? Turn it around and start remembering your dream. What has God put in your heart? What did you used to be excited about? Why do you think it's too late, it's too big, it's not possible? Get your passion back. You're not lacking, and you didn't get shortchanged.

Everything You Need

Since we have gifts that differ according to the grace given to us, each of us is to use them accordingly.

Romans 12:6 AMP

When God breathed His life into you, He put in you everything you need to fulfill your destiny. The Most High God is on your side. You have royal blood flowing through your veins. There are dreams in you so big that you can't accomplish them on your own. It's going to take you connecting with your Creator, knowing that God is directing your steps. But you have to stir up your gift. The enemy would love for you to keep your dream buried and wants to convince you that it's never going to happen, that it's too late. Don't believe those lies. You can still become all you were created to be. Every time you remember your dream, every time you say, "Lord, thank You for bringing it to pass," you're removing some dirt. You're digging it out.

Words of Faith

*"Let the weak say,
'I am strong.'"*

Joel 3:10 NKJV

Maybe you've been dealing with an illness for a long time. Early on you believed you would get well, but now you've just learned to live with it. What's happened is that your healing, your breakthrough, your freedom have gotten buried. They're still in you; they're still alive. But when you're thinking, *It will never happen. I've had so many negative reports*, that's burying it deeper. Why don't you get your shovel out and start removing the dirt? How do you do that? Say, "Lord, thank You that You're restoring health to me. Thank You that I'm free from this addiction, free from this depression." If you'll keep talking like that, the dream that's been buried will come back to life. That's what allows God to do great things. He's moved by our faith, not by our doubts, discouragement, or complaining.

Bring It to Life

*"A good man out of the good treasure of
his heart brings forth good things."*

Matthew 12:35 NKJV

As long as you dwell on past hurts, you're going to get stuck. "But Joel, I'll never meet the right person. I've been hurt too many times." You're remembering the wrong thing. Start remembering the dream. "Lord, You said that You would bring the perfect person into my life, somebody better than I ever imagined." Stop saying, "I could never accomplish my goal. I'll never get this promotion. I don't have the talent. I've tried, but I always get passed over." That's burying the dream, putting more dirt on it. You need to get a shovel and start digging that dream out. You may have been doing this for so long that you need a backhoe. You need some heavy equipment because it's buried way down deep in the darkness. You can dig it up and bring it to life.

Wake Up

Awake, awake, Zion, clothe yourself with strength! Put on your garments of splendor, Jerusalem, the holy city.

Isaiah 52:1

Whatever dream that God has put in you, no matter how long it's been, no matter how impossible it looks, I'm asking you to stir it up. It starts in your thinking, in what you're believing, and in what you're saying. No more "It's never going to happen." No, you have to say, "I'm surrounded by God's favor. Blessings are chasing me down. Because I delight myself in the Lord, He will give me the desires of my heart." Get in agreement with God. He's the giver of all dreams. He's the one who put that desire in you. You may need to get alone, be quiet, and search your heart. Say to Him, "God, anything that I've pushed down, anything that I've given up on, show me what it is. Don't let me die with any dreams still buried."

DECEMBER

1

Go Up at Once

Then Caleb quieted the people before Moses, and said, "Let us go up at once and take possession, for we are well able to overcome it."

Numbers 13:30 NKJV

God put a dream into Caleb's heart for the people of Israel to go into the Promised Land at once, but his dream was buried because the other people believed a negative report. The Israelites were camped next door to the Promised Land, but they turned around, and that group of people never went in. I can imagine Caleb was discouraged. He knew they were supposed to go in. God put that dream in his heart, but it didn't happen. It looked as though the other people had kept him from his destiny. Most people would have given up and settled where they were, but not Caleb. The true mark of a champion is that even when some dirt gets thrown on a dream, they keep looking for new ways to move forward, believing for new opportunities.

Conquer That Mountain

*"Now give me this hill country
that the LORD promised
me that day."*

Joshua 14:12

Forty years after God gave Caleb the dream
to go into the Promised Land, when he
was eighty-five years old, he could still feel this
dream stirring inside. He wasn't sitting around
feeling sorry for himself, saying, "I really tried.
If only those other people had done what was
right." At eighty-five Caleb went back to that
same mountain where the others refused to
go, and he said, "Give me this mountain!"
What's significant is that there were three
giants living on that mountain—three
Goliaths. I can hear a friend say, "Come on,
Caleb, you're eighty-five. Here, take this easy
mountain instead." He would have said, "No,
thanks. I'm not going to settle for mediocrity
when God has placed greatness in me. I want
that mountain." He went and conquered the
mountain that God had promised him. The
dream came to pass.

December 3

Destiny Calls

May he give you the desire of your heart
and make all your plans succeed.

Psalm 20:4

Have you allowed any dreams to get buried in you? At one time you thought you could do something great, but that was a long time ago. You had some bad breaks that weren't your fault. You have a good excuse to settle; nobody would blame you if you did. But God sent me to light a fire inside you. That dream is still alive. You may have tried to make it happen a year ago, or five years ago, or forty years ago, but it didn't work out. God is saying to you, "Go back and try again. This is your time. This is your moment. Your destiny is calling out to you." You can't have a give-up spirit and take the easy way out. Don't settle for less than your dream and refuse to enter the struggle. Your destiny is at stake!

December 4

Your Heart's Desire

*You have granted him his heart's desire and have
not withheld the request of his lips.*

Psalm 21:2

I read about a little boy who grew up with a
desire to be a writer but was raised in a very
dysfunctional home. At fifteen he dropped
out of school, having never learned how to
read or write. He started drinking, and for
thirty-five years that's all he did. But one day
he told his buddies he'd never take another
drink of alcohol, and that day he was set
free. At fifty-one years old he went back to
school, learned how to read and write, and
earned his diploma. Then he started writing
poetry. He was a very gifted, eloquent writer.
That dream had been buried deep under
dysfunction and addictions, but it was still
alive. At seventy-five years old, he continues
to write and inspire people, letting them
know that it's never too late to accomplish
their dreams.

Like a Fire

5

But if I say, "I will not mention his word or speak anymore in his name," his word is in my heart like a fire, a fire shut up in my bones.

Jeremiah 20:9

What you wanted to do earlier in life didn't go away just because it didn't work. It's still in you. When the prophet Jeremiah was so discouraged by being persecuted and mocked for speaking God's word that you thought he was going to quit, he suddenly said, "But His word is like a burning fire shut up in my bones." I believe there are some dreams shut up in you that are like a fire. You tried to get away from it when it didn't work out the first time, but this is a new day. You may have missed some opportunities, but God knows how to make up for lost time. He says, "I will restore to you the years" (Joel 2:25). You may have lost years, but God can still get you to where you're supposed to be.

Hold to Your Dream

Then they said to one another, "Look, this dreamer is coming!"

Genesis 37:19 NKJV

Some people can't handle and won't celebrate what God has put in you. For instance, God gave Joseph a dream, but his brothers got jealous of him and were going to kill him. When he walked up, one of them said sarcastically, "Here comes the dreamer." In the past the brothers had been upset because Joseph was their father's favored son, but now they were even more upset because he'd had a dream. They were offended because he was determined to do something greater than what they had done, to leave his mark. They would have been fine if he were content to be average, to accept the status quo. But when you stir up what God has put in you, when you believe that you have seeds of greatness, let me warn you that not everybody will celebrate you.

Not Your Battle

"Thus says the LORD to you: 'Do not be afraid nor dismayed because of this great multitude, for the battle is not yours, but God's.'"

2 Chronicles 20:15 NKJV

When you have a dream, you're going to have some detractors. When you believe that you can pay off your house, start a business, or be successful in spite of past mistakes, some people will become jealous and try to make you look bad or try to talk you out of it. "Do you really think you'll get that promotion? You don't have the experience." "Do you really think you'll meet the right person? It didn't work out the last three times you tried." Let that go in one ear and out the other. The critics, the naysayers, and the haters don't control your destiny. God does. They can't keep you from your dreams. They may do something that puts you at a disadvantage, but God knows how to take what was meant for your harm and use it to promote you.

Let Them Go

DECEMBER 8

"Anyone who wants to be my follower must love me far more than he does his own father, mother, wife, children, brothers, or sisters…"

Luke 14:26 TLB

Joseph's own brothers tried to push his dream down. I say this respectfully, but sometimes your relatives won't celebrate you. Sometimes the people closest to you will be the least supportive. Here's the key: don't get distracted with fighting battles that don't matter, trying to prove to them who you are, trying to convince them to believe in you. You don't need their approval. You have Almighty God's approval. Let them go. What stirs them up is the fact that you're moving forward, pursuing your destiny. They want you to keep your dream buried in a dark place so you don't rise higher and make them look bad. Successful people, people who have and pursue a dream, don't waste their time looking at what everybody else is doing. They're too busy focusing on what God has put in their hearts.

Focus on Your Goal

*"I am doing a great work and I cannot come down.
Why should the work stop while I leave it and
come down to you [the opposition]?"*

Nehemiah 6:3 ESV

The enemy targets people who have a dream, who know that nothing is impossible because they believe. He'll use opposition, delays, discouragement, jealousy, and everything else he can to try to convince you to bury that dream. If you're going to reach your full potential, you have to make up your mind that you are in it for the long haul. You're not going to let people talk you out of it. You're not going to let circumstances discourage you, or let delays cause you to give up, or let critical people get you distracted. You stay focused on your goal. Here's the key: you wouldn't have that opposition if you didn't have something great in you. If that dream weren't alive and on track, right on schedule to come to pass, you wouldn't have so many things coming against you.

Abundant Life

"I came so they can have real and eternal life,
more and better life than they ever dreamed of."

John 10:10 MSG

When you're a dreamer, you're dangerous to the enemy. He knows that you're headed for new levels. He knows that you're going to set a new standard for your family. He knows that you're coming into abundance. And he knows that there's nothing he can do to stop you. The forces that are for you are greater than the forces that are against you. But he'll work overtime to try to convince you to settle where you are. You have to remember this principle: when negative things happen, they cannot stop your destiny; they are a sign that you're on the way to your destiny. Those bad breaks are all a part of the process. The delay, the people who did you wrong, or the time it didn't work out is just another step on the way to your destiny.

Remember the Promise

11

Then Joseph remembered the dreams which he had dreamed about them...

Genesis 42:9 NKJV

When Joseph's brothers, who had sold him into slavery and caused him years of pain, showed up at the Egyptian palace looking to purchase food, they didn't realize they were standing in front of him. You would think that Joseph would be bitter and vindictive. This was his chance to pay them back, and he had the power to do it. But when Joseph saw his brothers, he remembered his dream. He didn't remember the hurt or the betrayal. As they bowed down before him, he remembered the promise that God had spoken to him. All those bad breaks he had suffered through, all that time when it looked as though he had missed his destiny—the whole time God was in control. It was meant for his harm, but God turned it around and used it for his good.

Fulfillment of the Promise

"Blessed is she who believed, for there will be a fulfillment of those things which were told her from the Lord."

Luke 1:45 NKJV

When God gives you a dream, when He puts a promise in your heart, that doesn't mean it's going to come to pass without opposition, delays, and adversities. You'll have plenty of opportunities to get discouraged and frustrated, thinking it's never going to happen. In the tough times you have to remember your dream as Joseph did. God didn't bring you this far to leave you. Stay in faith and keep a good attitude. Let God be your vindicator. "Well, Joel, I'm in the pits. This is a dark place. I don't understand it." Don't worry, because a caravan is coming to move you to your next location. "A friend lied about me." "I went through a divorce." Don't get bitter. It's just a detour on the way to your destiny. The palace is coming. The promise is still on track.

December 13

Glory Is Permanent

*For our light affliction, which is but for a
moment, is working for us a far more exceeding
and eternal weight of glory.*

2 Corinthians 4:17 NKJV

When you face opposition and things
don't go your way, recognize that it's not
permanent. That's not your final destination.
Quit worrying about things that are only
temporary—the betrayal, the injustice, the
loneliness. That's not your permanent home.
It's a temporary stop. The psalmist wrote
of "passing through the Valley of Weeping"
(Ps. 84:6 AMP), not "settling in the Valley of
Weeping," or "getting stuck in the Valley," or
"building a house in the Valley." The Valley
is temporary; you're passing through it. Now
my challenge is to quit losing sleep over a
temporary stop. Quit being stressed out
over something that's only for a season; it's
not permanent. The right people, the right
opportunities, the healing, the vindication, the
restoration are headed your way. The affliction
is temporary, but the glory is permanent.

December 14

Refreshing Springs

When they walk through the Valley of Weeping,
it will become a place of refreshing springs.

Psalm 84:6 NLT

You may have a dream that you've buried and given up on. You need to get your shovel out and start thanking God that it's coming to pass. Stir up what's on the inside. Maybe you're on a detour right now, going through something you don't understand. Don't get discouraged. You're just passing through. It's easy to remember the hurt and the disappointment. I'm asking you to remember the dream, remember the promise. If you do this, I believe that dreams you've buried will come back to life. Promises that you've given up on will be resurrected. Your time is coming. As He did with Joseph, God is going to turn every stumbling block into a stepping-stone. You will rise higher, accomplish your goals, and become everything you were created to be.

15

An Expected End

For I know the thoughts that I think toward you, saith the LORD, thoughts of peace, and not of evil, to give you an expected end.

Jeremiah 29:11 KJV

I once asked a well-known actor who also writes movies, "How do you know where to start?" He said, "You always start with your final scene. Once you establish how you want the movie to end, you work backward and fill in all the details."

This is what God has done for each one of us. The prophet Isaiah said that God declares "the end from the beginning" (Isa. 46:10 NKJV). When God planned out your life, He started with where He wants you to end up, and then He worked backward. His plans for you are "to give you an expected end." The good news is that you end in victory, fulfilling your destiny. You can live in peace, knowing that in the end, all things are going to work to your advantage.

Planned Long Ago

For we are God's masterpiece. He has created us anew in Christ Jesus, so we can do the good things he planned for us long ago.

Ephesians 2:10 NLT

As in a movie, there will be twists and turns in your life story. There will be scenes in your life that on their own don't make sense. If you stopped right there at the divorce, the sickness, or the loss, it would look as though things didn't work out, as though a dream has died. You may be in a difficult scene right now, but that's not your final scene, and that's not how your story ends. You have an expected end. The Creator of the universe, the Most High God, has already planned it for good and not harm. If you'll keep moving forward, there's going to be another twist coming, but this time it will be a good break, a promotion, a restoration, a healing. God knows how to weave it all together. He's already established the end.

Tested by Fire

…so that the tested genuineness of your faith— more precious than gold that perishes though it is tested by fire—may be found to result in praise…

1 Peter 1:7 ESV

God destined Joseph to become a ruler in Egypt so he could help his family and the world in a time of widespread famine. That was the end. It was established. Joseph started off well, but his story took several unusually dark twists—from being sold into slavery to being put in prison for something that he hadn't done. He could have thought, *God gave me a dream that my family would bow down to me, but it sure didn't work out.* But Joseph knew his end had been set, so he just kept being his best.

This is the real test of faith. Will you keep a good attitude when you're doing the right thing but the wrong thing is happening, knowing that your end is established?

Paths of Peace

"...to give light to those who sit in darkness and in the shadow of death, and to guide us to the path of peace."

Luke 1:79 TLB

DECEMBER 18

When so many things went wrong in Joseph's life, he didn't fall apart and become bitter. He just kept doing the right thing, and he finally made it to the palace throne. If Joseph were here today, he would say, "Don't get discouraged by the detours, the strange twists, and the dark scenes that don't make sense on their own. God knows how to weave it all together, and in the end you'll come out fulfilling your purpose, seeing what He promised."

Something may look as though it is there to defeat you, but God is going to use it to increase you. No bad break can stop you. All the forces of darkness cannot hold you down. God has an expected end for you; He's already established it.

Taken Higher

From the ends of the earth I call to you,
I call as my heart grows faint; lead me to
the rock that is higher than I.

Psalm 61:2

Many people get frustrated and soured on life because of their unanswered whys. You may never understand why something happened the way it did, but God wouldn't have allowed it if it weren't going to somehow work for your good. Nothing that's happened to you can keep you from your destiny. The only thing that can stop you is you. If you get negative and bitter and lose your passion, that's going to keep you from God's best. You may have had unfair things happen to you, but I've learned that the depth of your pain is an indication of the height of your future. The taller the building, the deeper the foundation. When you go through difficulties and unfair situations, God is getting you prepared to be taken higher than you ever imagined.

Created to Be

*Put on your new nature, created to be like God—
truly righteous and holy.*

Ephesians 4:24 NLT

Not everything along your life's way is going to make sense. This is where faith comes in. You have to trust that even in the scenes that you don't understand, in the twists of life, God knows what He's doing. As was true of Joseph, you know that God promised you one thing—influence, leadership, new levels—but that everything that's happening indicates just the opposite—defeat, betrayal, insignificance. When you come to a dead end with something you don't understand, that's when you have to dig your heels in and say, "God, I don't understand it, but I trust in You. I believe that Your plans for me are for good. I believe that You've already set my end and shot my final scene. I believe that I will fulfill my purpose and become who You created me to be."

A Full Warranty

21

God's gifts and God's call are under full warranty—never canceled, never rescinded.

Romans 11:29 MSG

I've heard it said that God always ends in "all is well." If all is not well, that means it's not the end. "Joel, it's not well in my finances. I'm struggling." Don't get discouraged; it's not the end. That's just one scene. Favor is coming. Breakthroughs are coming. Abundance is coming. Maybe it's not well in a relationship—you went through a breakup, you're lonely, and you don't think you'll ever meet the right person. It's not the end. The person who left didn't stop God's plan or change His ending. They don't have that kind of power. God has already established your ending. He's already lined up the person of your dreams, somebody better than you ever imagined. They're just a couple scenes away. It's just a matter of time before that person shows up.

Life Purpose

"For the LORD of hosts has purposed, and who will annul it?"

Isaiah 14:27 NKJV

God has a purpose for your life. He's already planned out your days, lined up the different scenes, and established your ending. Then it asks, "Who can stop it?" God is saying, "I'm the all-powerful Creator of the universe. Now, who can change your ending? People can't, unfair situations can't, tragedy can't. I have the final say." When all the scenes of your life come together, it's going to work out for your good. If Joseph hadn't been betrayed by his brothers, hadn't been sold into slavery, hadn't been falsely accused and put into prison, he wouldn't have made it to the throne. Those were all necessary scenes on the way to his established ending. What am I saying? What looks like a setback is really God setting you up to get you to the fullness of your destiny.

December 23

Always to Triumph

*Now thanks be to God who always
leads us in triumph...*

2 Corinthians 2:14 NKJV

One day I recorded an important basketball
game that I knew I was going to miss.
The next week I sat down to watch it. I
already knew our team had won from news
reports. My team couldn't do anything right
and fell behind, then further behind into the
second half. Normally I would have been on
edge and anxious, but because I knew the
outcome, I didn't get the least bit worried.
In fact, the further behind we fell, the more
I thought, *This is going to be an exciting
comeback. I can't wait to see what happens.*

Just as with that basketball game, you
have to remind yourself that the end has
been set. God said, "I always cause you to
triumph." He's already lined up the victory
parade.

Peace at All Times

Now may the Lord of peace himself give
you peace at all times and in every way.
The Lord be with all of you.

2 Thessalonians 3:16

In life there are times when it looks as though our opponents—the sickness, the depression, the loss—are getting the best of us. It's easy to get discouraged. You can go through life fighting everything that doesn't go your way, being worried, negative, and upset. Or you can stay in peace, knowing that God is directing your steps, even the detours and the dead ends. You have to remind yourself that the end has been set. When it feels as though you're far behind, outnumbered, outsized, and outclassed, instead of being discouraged, have a new perspective. That means you're about to see a major comeback. At any moment things are going to shift in your favor. A good break, a healing, a promotion, or a restoration is coming. God has the final say. He's already shot your final scene.

Finish Well

25

The end of a matter is better than its beginning, and patience is better than pride.

Ecclesiastes 7:8

A friend of mine was raised in a very dysfunctional home. His father died when he was four years old. When he was eleven years old, his mother abandoned him on a street corner and for three days he waited there—confused, hungry, and afraid. A man noticed him, asked if he needed help, and then this man and his wife took him into their home and eventually adopted him. As he grew up, this young man had a desire to help other children in at-risk environments and began to bring needy children to Sunday school. Today this man's ministry has grown to reach 150,000 children every week, letting them know that they too can do something great in life. You may have had a rough start, but you're not going to have a rough finish. God has already established the end.

Leave Your Mark

Neither before nor after Josiah was there a king like him who turned to the LORD as he did—with all his heart and with all his soul...

2 Kings 23:25

How you start is not important. Don't let what you think is a disadvantage or a bad break cause you to say, "If I'd had a better childhood, if I had more support, if I didn't have this dysfunction, I could do something great." That's where you started, but that's not where you're going to finish. The beginning doesn't determine your destiny. That's just one scene. What matters is the expected end. The Creator of the universe has already destined you to leave your mark. He's already put seeds of greatness in you. If you'll keep honoring God and being your best, you're moving toward the purpose God has designed for you. He loves to take people who start with the odds against them and shine down His favor, give them breaks, increase them, and cause them to do extraordinary things.

A Flourishing Finish

God who started this great work in you would keep at it and bring it to a flourishing finish on the very day Christ Jesus appears.

Philippians 1:6 MSG

The apostle Paul did not say that God will bring you "to a defeated finish," "an unfair finish," "a lonely finish," or a "bankrupt finish." God has a victorious finish, an abundant finish, "a flourishing finish." When those thoughts tell you, "It's never going to work out. You have too many disadvantages, and you've made too many mistakes," let those lies go in one ear and out the other. God has established the end, and He knows how to get you there. Now all through the day, just say, "Lord, I want to thank You that Your plans for me are for good. I may not understand everything along the way, and it may not have been fair, but I'm not going to live worried, upset, or discouraged. I know You're bringing me to a flourishing finish."

Still Enthroned

"For I know that my Redeemer lives…"

Job 19:25 NKJV

Nearly overnight Job's life was shattered by great personal losses and covered in darkness. He could have given up on his faith. Even his wife told him, "Job, just curse God and die. You're done." In the midst of the difficulty, Job looked up to the heavens and said, "I know that my Redeemer lives." He was saying, in effect, "I know God is still on the throne. He's already established my end. I'm not going to get bitter or upset. Though He slay me, yet will I trust Him." When you can give God praise when life doesn't make sense, God will release you into a new level of your destiny. When you don't let the strange twists and the things that you don't understand cause you to get sour, you pass the test and will see your established end.

After This

After this, Job lived a hundred and forty years; he saw his children and their children to the fourth generation.

Job 42:16

We hear a lot about Job's trials, Job's suffering, and Job's loss. Yes, he went through a difficult season of darkness, but he didn't stay there. In the end he came out with twice what he'd had before. Scripture says that after this Job lived for another 140 blessed years.

Notice that after the difficulty, his life was not over, and he didn't end on a sour, defeated note. Just because you experience a twist, a detour, or a setback doesn't mean your life is over. God has an *after this* coming. When you go through tough times, He's not only going to bring you out, He's going to pay you back for that trouble. You're going to come out increased, promoted, and better than you were before.

Already Established

*Job answered GOD: "I'm convinced: You can
do anything and everything. Nothing and
no one can upset your plans."*

Job 42:2 MSG

After all Job had endured, he was saying
that the expected end cannot be
changed. The Scripture talks about how
Satan had to ask for permission to test Job.
The enemy can't do anything he wants; he
has to get God's permission to touch you.
God is not only in control of your life, He's
in control of your enemies. You have nothing
to worry about. He has a hedge of protection
around you that cannot be penetrated.

Perhaps you hear thoughts whispering,
*You'll never be as happy again. You've seen
your best days.* Don't believe those lies. You
haven't laughed your best laugh, you haven't
dreamed your best dream, you haven't danced
your best dance, and you haven't sung your
best song. God has already established your
expected end.

DECEMBER

31

Keep Looking Ahead

Jesus answered them, "Destroy this temple, and I will raise it again in three days."

John 2:19

Jesus said this when He was about to be crucified, people thought He was talking about the building, but He was talking about Himself. He knew that His end had been established. His final scene was not one of being betrayed and mistreated, hanging on a cross in great pain, or being buried in a tomb wrapped up in grave clothes. He knew that His final scene was that of being seated at the right hand of His Father, with all power, with the keys of death and hell. That's why Scripture says, "For the joy that was set before Him endured the cross, scorning its shame" (Heb. 12:2). In the tough times, the way to keep your joy is to keep looking ahead, knowing that you will have a flourishing finish, knowing that God always causes you to triumph.

Stay connected, be blessed.

From thoughtful articles to powerful blogs, podcasts and more, JoelOsteen.com is full of inspirations that will give you encouragement and confidence in your daily life.

Visit us today at JoelOsteen.com.

Hope is on the move!

Watch messages, read our free daily devotional and more! Inspiration is always at your fingertips with the free Joel Osteen app for iPhone and Android.

CONNECT WITH US
Join our community of believers on your favorite social network

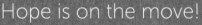

Thanks for helping us make a difference in the lives of millions around the world.

Notes

Notes

Notes